BMW
CUSTOM MOTORCYCLES

Choppers, Cruisers,
Bobbers, Trikes &
Quads

Also from Veloce –

Speedpro Series
Harley-Davidson Evolution Engines – How to Build & Power Tune (Hammill)

Those Were The Days ... Series
Café Racer Phenomenon, The (Walker)
Drag Bike Racing in Britain – From the mid '60s to the mid '80s (Lee)
Three Wheelers (Bobbitt)

Enthusiast's Restoration Manual Series
Yamaha FS1-E, How to Restore (Watts)

Essential Buyer's Guide Series
BMW GS (Henshaw)
BSA Bantam (Henshaw)
BSA 500 & 650 Twins (Henshaw)
Harley-Davidson Big Twins (Henshaw)
Hinckley Triumph triples & fours 750, 900, 955, 1000, 1050, 1200 – 1991-2009 (Henshaw)
Honda CBR600 (Henshaw)
Honda FireBlade (Henshaw)
Honda SOHC fours 1969-1984 (Henshaw)
Norton Commando (Henshaw)
Triumph Bonneville (Henshaw)
Vespa Scooters – Classic 2-stroke models 1960-2008 (Paxton)

Biographies
Edward Turner: The Man Behind the Motorcycles (Clew)
Jim Redman – 6 Times World Motorcycle Champion: The Autobiography (Redman)

General
BMW Boxer Twins 1970-1996 Bible, The (Falloon)
Caring for your 50cc Scooter – Your guide to maintenance & safety checks (Fry)

Ducati 750 Bible, The (Falloon)
Ducati 750 SS 'round-case' 1974, The Book of the (Falloon)
Ducati 860, 900 and Mille Bible, The (Falloon)
Ducati Monster Bible, The (Falloon)
Fine Art of the Motorcycle Engine, The (Peirce)
Funky Mopeds (Skelton)
Kawasaki Triples Bible, The (Walker)
Lambretta Bible, The (Davies)
Laverda Twins & Triples Bible 1968-1986 (Falloon)
Moto Guzzi Sport & Le Mans Bible, The (Falloon)
Motorcycle Apprentice (Cakebread)
Motorcycle Road & Racing Chassis Designs (Noakes)
MV Agusta Fours, The book of the (Falloon)
Scooter Lifestyle (Grainger)
Triumph Bonneville!, Save the – The inside story of the Meriden Workers' Co-op (Rosamond)
Triumph Motorcycles & the Meriden Factory (Hancox)
Triumph Speed Twin & Thunderbird Bible (Woolridge)
Triumph Tiger Cub Bible (Estall)
Triumph Trophy Bible (Woolridge)
Velocette Motorcycles – MSS to Thruxton New Third Edition (Burris)

From Veloce Publishing's new imprints:

Battle Cry!
Soviet General & field rank officer uniforms: 1955 to 1991 (Streather)
Red & Soviet military & paramilitary services: female uniforms 1941-1991 (Streather)

Hubble & Hattie
Animal Grief – How animals mourn for each other (Alderton)

Clever Dog! (O'Meara)
Complete Dog Massage Manual, The – Gentle Dog Care (Robertson)
Dinner with Rover (Paton-Ayre)
Dog Cookies (Schops)
Dog Games – Stimulating play to entertain your dog and you (Blenski)
Dogs on wheels (Mort)
Dog Relax – Relaxed dogs, relaxed owners (Pilguj)
Exercising your puppy: a gentle & natural approach – Gentle Dog Care (Robertson)
Fun and games for cats (Seidl)
Know Your Dog – The guide to a beautiful relationship (Birmelin)
Living with an Older Dog – Gentle Dog Care (Alderton & Hall)
My dog has cruciate ligament injury – but lives life to the full! (Häusler)
My dog has hip dysplasia – but lives life to the full! (Häusler)
My dog is blind – but lives life to the full! (Horsky)
My dog is deaf – but lives life to the full! (Willms)
Smellorama – nose games for dogs (Theby)
Swim to Recovery: Canine hydrotherapy healing (Wong)
Waggy Tails & Wheelchairs (Epp)
Walking the dog – motorway walks for drivers and dogs (Rees)
Winston ... the dog who changed my life (Klute)
You and Your Border Terrier – The Essential Guide (Alderton)
You and Your Cockapoo – The Essential Guide (Alderton)

www.veloce.co.uk

First published in April 2011 by Veloce Publishing Limited, Veloce House, Parkway Farm Business Park, Middle Farm Way, Poundbury, Dorchester, Dorset, DT1 3AR, England.
Fax 01305 250479/e-mail info@veloce.co.uk/web www.veloce.co.uk or www.velocebooks.com.

ISBN: 978-1-845843-25-0 UPC: 6-36847-04325-4

Readers with ideas for automotive books, or books on other transport or related hobby subjects, are invited to write to the editorial director of Veloce Publishing at the above address.
British Library Cataloguing in Publication Data – A catalogue record for this book is available from the British Library.
Typesetting, design and page make-up all by Veloce Publishing Ltd on Apple Mac. Printed in India by Replika Press.

BMW
CUSTOM MOTORCYCLES

Choppers, Cruisers,
Bobbers, Trikes &
Quads

VELOCE PUBLISHING
THE PUBLISHER OF FINE AUTOMOTIVE BOOKS

Contents

Foreword

—

I like motorcycles. In fact, I'm obsessed with them. Ever since I saw a Norton Commando overtake my parents' car on a German motorway when I was a young lad, they have fascinated me. I find their combination of power, sound and aesthetics very appealing.

I have owned a few different brands and styles of bikes over the years, but I always return to BMW. There is something about these bikes that draws me back to them. It is said a BMW is not just for show, it is meant for riding. My last airhead BMW was 30 years old when I sold it recently. It had 121,500 miles on the clock and never missed a beat, never let me down.

So, why use a BMW motorcycle engine (and its derivatives) in a chopper, cruiser, or bobber? Really, the question is – why not? There have always been chops on the road with engines that don't follow the vee-twin route, especially in Europe. The Harley engine doesn't own the chop genre, although it dominates the market. BMW and Ural engines are used in choppers and bobbers in some parts of Europe for cost and availability reasons, as in former Eastern bloc countries. Others use this machinery because they were convinced of its reliability and engineering, while others just wanted to be different.

It was only private individuals and bike shop owners that built BMW chops until June 1997, when the BMW factory decided to bring its very own cruiser onto the market. Some loved the styling, others hated it, but it was a bold and fresh move for the factory to enter a new market sector. The bike sold well for some years, cashing in on the soaring popularity of the cruiser market, especially in the USA and Germany. However, after some time, the Japanese manufacturers began churning out larger and larger cruiser engines. BMW could not keep pace with this competition – its boxer engine design struggled to go beyond 1200cc. Subsequently, BMW withdrew from this market.

But wait, this is not the last we see of the BMW factory, or of individuals building BMW choppers, cruisers or bobbers. Hendrik von Kuenheim, the BMW general director, was quoted in the British *Motorcycle News* in 2008: "I hate the word cruiser because it identifies with Harley ... We have an 85-year history of boxers and I believe we are obliged to go our own way, so we can be proud of what we have ... the last thing we want is to be considered a knock off." He introduced the BMW Lo Rider concept bike at the Milan Bike Show in November 2008. This machine was enthusiastically received by the public, and it is now being considered for future production. Watch this space!

As well as cruisers, choppers, et al, this book also features a selection of creatively crafted trikes and quads to round up the picture. I hope you enjoy seeing all the amazing bikes as much as I enjoyed bringing it all together. Ride on!

Uli Cloesen

Introduction

The purpose of this book is to showcase BMW-powered (and BMW derivatives) customised machinery in one place. It is not intended to reinvent the wheel in terms of what has already been published about BMW motorcycles or chopper and bobber bikes. The collection of illustrations presented is simply a window to what's out there.

Life would be boring without a touch of individuality, creativity, and flair. This applies even more so to two-, three- or four-wheeled transport/leisure vehicles. There has to be an emotional response, a feel-good factor in engaging us to build, ride, or drive.

So, what triggered the invention of the bobber? When US soldiers returned home after World War II, they wanted bikes more like the European ones they had seen, motorcycles with less bulk than their homegrown types.

A bobber was created by shedding – or 'bobbing' – weight, particularly by scrapping the front fender and shortening the rear fender, with the intention of making the bike lighter and faster. (NB not all countries allow the removal of fenders on bikes.) A more minimalist ride was perceived to look better than the then standard machines.

It wasn't until 1969, and the appearance of American road movie *Easy Rider*, starring Peter Fonda, Dennis Hopper and Jack Nicholson, that the term 'chopper' arrived on the scene. Motorcycle enthusiasts again found new ways to modify their bikes. People started changing the angle of the front forks, reducing the size of the gas tank, and adding ape hanger handlebars to their bikes. To round it off, a thin front wheel and a large rear tire were added to the package.

The main difference between bobbers and choppers is that the former are usually built around standard frames, while the frames of the latter are often cut and welded to suit. Bobbers also often lack chromed parts and long forks.

Cruiser is the term for bikes that copy the style of American machines like Harley or Indian. This sector of the motorcycle market is most popular in the United States. The big four bike manufacturers – Honda, Kawasaki, Suzuki and Yamaha – all produced Harley clones for this very important market. Riding on a cruiser typically entails a feet-forward riding position with an upright body. The low-slung design of this type of bike limits its cornering ability – chopper motorcycles are considered cruisers in this context.

A trike is, in essence, a three-wheeled motorcycle. If you don't like the idea of riding a bike, but are after the thrilling acceleration and speed of one, with the safety of an added wheel, this might be the vehicle for you. In many countries you don't have to wear a helmet when riding a trike, because they can be registered like a car.

The quad started three decades ago with the Honda US90, the first all-terrain vehicle (ATV). Less expensive to run than a utility truck or tractor, smaller and more maneuverable than either, and with low-pressure tires that were easy on sensitive ground, ATVs became essential tools in farming, and even as a means of mobility for the disabled.

As a departure from the ATV outline, there is a new branch of road-oriented quads with high-performance engines, some of them with chassis types leaning towards cars. Such quads are also explored in this book.

Uli Cloesen

Acknowledgements

The author and publisher wish to acknowledge their debt to all who loaned material and photographs for this book. Thank you, Alex, for encouraging me to do it all. Special thanks go to Dmitriy Khitrov and Koshey for helping me with contacts in the Russian bike scene, and to Joerg Schwertfechter in Germany. Thank you also to BMW New Zealand.

You are welcome to contact the author or publisher if you are interested in having your BMW chopper, cruiser, bobber, trike, or quad considered for inclusion in any future versions of this book.

CHAPTER 1

BMW SINGLES

MW single-cylinder motorcycles – specifically models R25 to R27, with plunger rear suspension and shaft final drive, built from 1950 to 1966 – have long been popular in Europe as a cheap route to customisation. Standard versions of these bikes are still used as daily transport in places like Greece and Turkey.

A good website for motorcycles of this type is www.bmw-einzylinder. de, the online meeting place for all BMW single vintage enthusiasts in Germany. Here, you can find instructions and information pertaining to single-cylinder models R23 to R27.

An original 250cc R25-2 from 1952, owned by Stefan Kettl in Germany.

Tobias Ehlers, Germany – BMW R25/3 conversion

Tobias brought this bike back to life after thirty years – not as an ordinary restoration, but in an old-school bobber style, while keeping the original parts. The machine is on the road again as of February 2009.

This bike, built in 1955, was de-registered in 1978.

ENGINE	
Designation	224/4
Type	Four-stroke single cylinder vertical
Bore x stroke	68 x 68mm (2.67 x 2.67in)
Displacement	247cc
Max power	13hp at 5800rpm
Compression ratio	7.0:1
Valves	OHV
Carburation	1 x Bing-type 1/24/41 or SAWE-type K24 F
Engine lubricating system	Forced feed lubrication
Oil pump	Gear pump

POWER TRANSMISSION	
Clutch	Single plate, dry
Number of gears	Four
Gearchange	Foot lever (& auxiliary manual lever)
Gearbox ratios	6.1/3.0/2.04/1.54
Final drive ratio	4.16:1 (with sidecar 4.8:1)
Bevel/crownwheel	6/25 teeth (with sidecar 5/24)

CHASSIS	
Designation	225/3
Frame	Closed steel twin loop, welded
Front wheel suspension	Telescopic fork
Rear wheel suspension	Telescopic

DIMENSIONS/WEIGHTS	
Length x width x height	2065 x 760 x 730mm
Wheelbase	1365mm/53.74in
Fuel tank capacity	12 litres/2.63 gal/3.17 gal US
Unladen weight with full tank	150kg/330lb
Fuel consumption	Approx 2.9 litres per 100km/ 97mpg/81mpg US
Oil consumption	Approx 0.7 litres per 1000km
Top speed	119kmph/73mph

The gas tank is from a Harley Sportster.

The original suspension is retained.

R25/3 bobber rear end.

BMW R25 chopper

Slavko Sekulic from www.airsekus.com in Serbia did the custom paint job for this bike 15 years ago.

BMW springer fork chopper from Serbia.

Typical long and low chopper style.

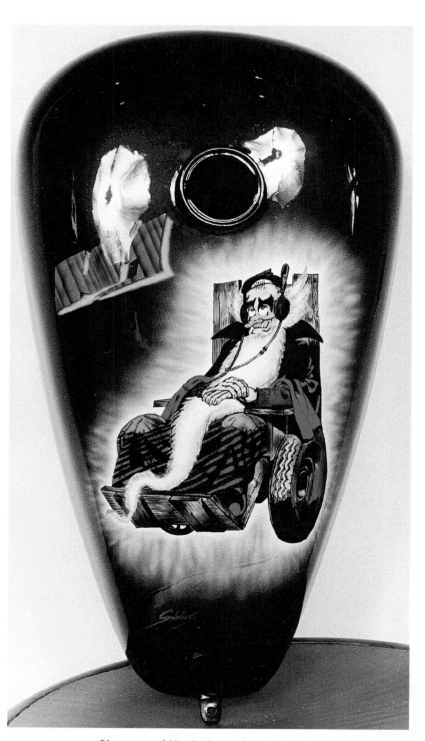

Close-up of Slavko's gas tank artwork.

Peter Scholl, Germany – BMW R25/3

The process of building this bike was a joint project carried out some time ago between three friends: Juergen, Jens (who provided the details) and Peter. Initially, Juergen – nicknamed 'Scheele' – owned the chopped R25/3, kitted out with a tiny, ultra-hard seat, forward controls, short drag bars and a 4-litre gas tank. One winter, the decision was made to dismantle and rebuild the bike. Scheele was a master at sourcing odd parts at swap meets, like an old seat that a bike could be built around, or a rear-view mirror with a 5cm diameter. The German TüV (Roadworthiness Authority) accepted the mirror, but asked him which budgie cage it was taken from! The bike received an 8-litre Harley Sportster tank after the frame rebuild, and SR500 handlebars on 8cm high risers. The trickiest part was fitting the seat low on the frame, while leaving enough comfort for the rider.

To get the desired appearance the fenders were chopped, and the rear light from a tractor fitted. Paintwise, it had to be black, and the blackest found was Porsche black gloss.

They were in for a surprise when, reconditioning the motor and gearbox, it became apparent that the cylinder head was from a BMW Isetta. This allowed the use of a Keihin carburettor from a Honda CX500, with a K&N air filter. The gearbox was from an R25/2 of 1949 vintage. Peter rewired the electrics and incorporated an ignition lock from a Honda monkey bike and an electronic ignition box. All this work was executed in a three-bedroom flat on the first floor, so the bike had to be coaxed down the staircase for its maiden run. After all this work, Scheele suddenly began worrying about all his other bikes and projects, and the bike changed hands to Peter.

Gearchanging technique had to be learned – there was no such thing as synchronization. Each gear change took two to three seconds at first, but after a week's training it worked like a dream.

The road-holding of this 50-year-old lady might be a bit wobbly compared to modern bikes, but is acceptable given the sedate

Gas tank sourced from a Harley Sportster.

A tidy BMW bobber.

The paint job is in Porsche black gloss.

The bike has Yamaha SR500 handlebars on 8cm high risers.

pace. Top speed and acceleration lose their importance with a bike like this. What counts is the single cylinder; you can count out each of the four strokes while riding. You ride at a comfortable pace through the landscape at 60 to 80kmph, and enjoy the surroundings and the sound of the exhaust. You are even greeted by farmers along the way, since you don't do 200kmph, and the chickens still have a chance to take off in time as the R25/3 approaches. Biker soul ... what more do you want? Going slow can be so cool.

GEDAECHTNIS MOPED
Builders/owners.. .. . Juergen Scheele [RIP 2003]
(idea, concept)
Jens Seehase (color, hardware)
Peter Scholl (owner, electrics, hardware)

Carburettor is from a Honda CX500.

Custom Art Orekvovo, Moscow

Sergey Kuzakov and Aleksandr Shiriaev, owners of the above-mentioned shop, built this chopper, called Pincher, based on a BMW R35 from 1939. The pair have built many choppers so far, and this bike is in Sergey's favourite style. Three basket cases were gathered together to get all the original engine parts. All the rest of the components were handmade and kept small to blend harmoniously with the small engine.

A beautiful, rigid-framed custom.

BMW PINCHER	
Builders/owners	Custom Art Orekhovo Moscow/ Kuzakov Sergey, Moscow, Russia
Engine	From BMW R35 – four-stroke overhead (1939) modified by Custom Art Orekhovo Moscow
Exhaust	Custom Art Orekhovo Moscow
Transmission.	EMW 1953 modified by Custom Art Orekhovo Moscow

Forks	Izh Orion Russian Motorcycle) – modified by Custom Art Orekhovo Moscow
Frame	Custom Art Orekhovo Moscow
Suspension	Custom Art Orekhovo Moscow
Gas tank.	Custom Art Orekhovo Moscow
Fenders	Custom Art Orekhovo Moscow
Seat	Custom Art Orekhovo Moscow
Wheels.	Front – 80/90-21, rear – 80/90-21 EMW
Special feature	Rigid frame, maximum speed 70kmph

Chopper Blues custom

This BMW R25/3 1955 was modified into a chopper by a friend from the BMW club, Jakarta. The photo below is from the club's 30th anniversary meeting. Changes from the original are:

CHOPPER BLUES	
Modified fork	Ex-Suzuki GTX 750
Wheel rim front and rear:	Ex-Honda Tiger/GL200, size 18in
Disc brake & hub	Kawasaki Ninja
Front mudguard	Handmade
Rear mudguard:	Modification from original part
Gas tank:	Handmade
Seat	Handmade
Fork cover	Handmade
Front lamp	Aftermarket
Electrics	Custom from 6 volt to 12 volt using custom car alternator
Carburation	Suzuki TS125 custom
Handlebars	Handmade

The wheels are laced with only 36 spokes to make the bike look lighter.

Stylish Moscow-built R35 chopper.

Chopper Blues. (Courtesy Pino from Indonesia)

CHAPTER 2
BMW AIRHEADS
(TWO-VALVE BOXERS)

BMW has an 85-year history of flat twin 'boxer'-engined bikes, and so this engine configuration has been the company's most recognized trademark to date.

A flat-twin is a two-cylinder engine with the horizontal cylinders arranged on opposite sides of the crankshaft. This geometry gives good primary balance, but creates an unbalanced moment on the crankshaft, caused by the pistons being offset from each other. The position of both cylinders protruding into the airflow allows excellent air cooling for each cylinder.

An original R51/3 twin from 1951.
(Courtesy Menoshire)

Part one: airhead choppers

These 1950s BMW R50 variants have long been a popular platform for chopper conversions.

Joerg Schwertfechter, Germany

Joerg discovered this bike in someone's garage many years ago, and just had to have it. It took four years of persuasion before the previous owner was finally willing to part with it, by which time, it wasn't in good shape anymore. Joerg completely dismantled the bike and rebuilt it from the ground up.

Owner..	Joerg Schwertfechter, Germany
Engine type..	R51/3, 500cc, 24hp
Seat height	0.64m
Forks..	BMW
Frame	Original, steering head stretched
Gas tank.	BCS
Seat	Custom-made
Wheels.	Front 3.25 x 19 ex-/5, rear 5.00 x 17
Special features	Chromed engine, gearbox, shaft, and forks

Joerg's R51/3.

The engine was chrome plated.

The steering head is stretched.

Joerg with his pride and joy.

This red chopper from Germany is owned by one of Joerg's friends ...

... the seat and paint job are classic 1970s.

BMW R51/3 from Holger Schwartz, Germany

This bike was built up by BC-Shop in Gummersbach in 1982. Holger has owned this chopper since 1992. A lot of effort went into chroming components and the custom paint job.

BMW 51/3 1952

Forks	Harley Davidson WLA 750 15 extended
Front wheel	3.25/19
Front brake	BSA drum
Rear wheel	5.00/16
Engine/gearbox	Chromed + gold leaf

Captain America-style BMW chopper.
(Courtesy J Schwertfechter)

The tank and frame received a white lacquer and gold leaf finish.
(Courtesy J Schwertfechter)

Engine with the full chrome treatment.
(Courtesy J Schwertfechter)

Fishtail exhaust complements the superb overall finish.
(Courtesy J Schwertfechter)

Emmanouil Ktistis, Rhodos, Greece

Emmanouil supplied me with these pictures of his 57-year-old blue beauty.

'Maltese cross' theme on the headlight and rear-view mirror.

Engine type..	Four-stroke, two-cylinder flat twin, 494cc
Exhaust	Fishtail 55cm
Transmission..	Four-speed, foot gearshift (and auxiliary manual lever on the gearbox), shaft drive 9/35 ratio
Electrical system	12V magneto ignition
Front fork..	Telescopic
Chassis.	Designation 251/4
Frame	Double loop steel tubular
Carburation	22in Dellorto phbl
Sparkplugs.	Bosch W4AC
Dimensions	2130 x 790 x 985mm
Gas tank.	Fat Bob-style
Fuel and capacity	Super 95 octane, 19 litres
Front fender	Plastic
Rear fender..	Steel two-piece handmade custom
Seat	Solo, leather, grey painted, iron cross
Seat height	72cm
Front wheel	90-90-18 with rims
Rear wheel	130-90-16 with rims
Front brake	200mm drum brake
Rear brake	200mm drum brake
Top speed	Approximately 120kmph

What better color for roaming around a Greek island?

The bike has a Fat Bob-style gas tank.

Emmanouil with Rhodos backdrop.

Markus (Leeroy) Wolff and Anette Engel-Wolff, Germany

Engine type	500cc, built 1965, 27hp
Exhaust	AME trumpets (www.ame-chopper.de)
Transmission	Four-speed, kick-start only
Forks	R75/5
Frame	R50

Gas tank	Mustang 12 litres
Fenders	Rear fender: AME
Seat	GTS (www.gts-seats.de)
Indicators	Bullseye
Wheels	Front 3.00/19 rear 5.00/16
Built	1969
Any special features	Registered as a BMW R50, all changes were signed of by the German TüV

The brown seat complements the bike's green paint job.

Close-up of the R50 engine.

This chopper was built by a friend of Markus' wife, according to her specification.

A fine example of German Rocker culture.

Markus (Leeroy) Wolff and Anette Engel-Wolff, Germany

This bike took Markus and a friend eight months to build. It is no longer owned by him.

The bike is registered as a BMW R50; all changes were signed off by the German TüV.

BMW R75 Fat Bob-style.

Engine type	800cc, 50hp, kick-start only
Exhaust	2-into-1 BSM
Transmission	Four-speed
Forks	R75/5
Chassis	R50 frame
Gas tank	Harley, 20 litres
Fenders	Rear homebuilt, Harley Fat Bob style
Seat	GTS (www.gts-seats.de)
Wheels	Front 3.00/19, rear 5.00/16
Indicators	Bullseye
Built	1969

The rear fender is home-made.

High-riser handlebars with bullseye indicators.

FNA Custom Cycles, Lakeland, Florida, USA

The boys from FNA created this custom with chain drive conversion. It's called Fat Herta. Eric tells the story:

"It started with my girl's dad having a stock '73 Beemer collecting dust in his barn, begging to be cut on. He didn't want to give it up to surgery but, long story short, we struck a deal, paid him the cash, gutted the bike, eBayed what we didn't need, and ended up with $130 profit. We started out with a few basic ideas: leaf spring front end, board-track bars, drop seat chassis, downdraft carburettors, and 23in front wheel. The engine was put in the frame jig, and we started bending tube around the motor.

The shaft to chain drive was adapted from an ATV differential with a brake rotor on one side, and sprocket extended on the other. The front end, rotor, fender strut and bearing carrier were designed using CAD, and then laser cut with Scotty's help. John cut up the stock tank and pieced it back together with Nate's welding help. The bars were bent after being packed with sand, and then welded by Nate and given back to John to put some shine on the stainless. We had a great time building, and now riding, the bike, but it still has some paint and polish to be done."

Owners	Eric Allard and John Mooney
City	Lakeland, Florida
Designer	FNA Custom Cycles

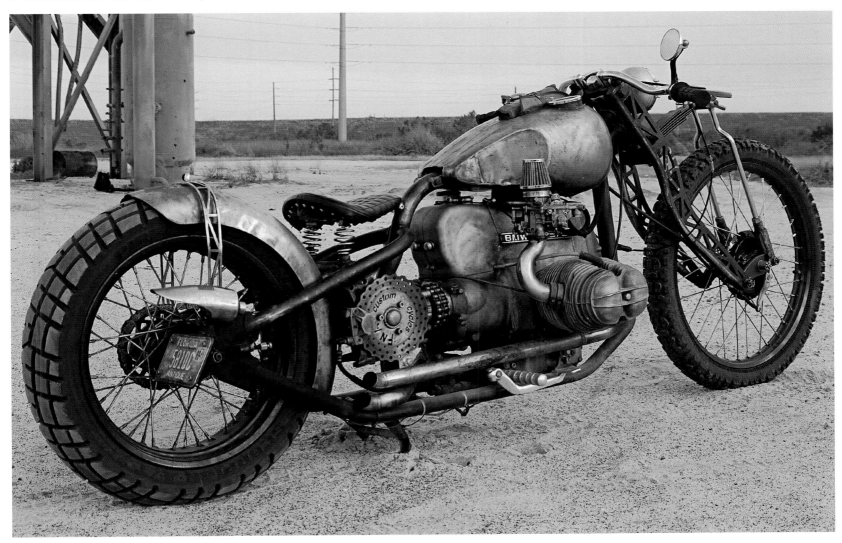

Fat Herta with industrial backdrop.

Leaf spring fork up-close.

GENERAL	
Fabrication	FNA
Year and make	1973 BMW/2009 FNA
Name	Fat Herta
Assembly	FNA
Time	8 months
Chroming	What's that?

FORKS	
Type	FNA leaf spring
Extension	Unknown
Builder	FNA Custom Cycles

The exhaust emits a hearty sound!

ENGINE

Year 1973
Model R75/5
Rebuilder . . . .David Bradshaw
Ignition. . . . .Points
Displacement 750cc
Lower end . . . .Stock
Balancing. . . . .Stock
Pistons . . . .Stock
Heads . . . .Stock
Cam. . . . .Stock
Lifters . . . .Stock
Carburation . . . .1982 Yamaha Vision 550
Air cleaners . . . .Triumph
Pipes . . . .FNA custom SS
Mufflers . . . .Huh?
Transmission. . . . .BMW four-speed
Modifications . . . .Chain-drive conversion with custom diff
Gearshift. . . . .Left foot

PAINTING

Painter . . . . Thompson's Auto Body
Color/type. . . . . Naked steel
Special paint . . . . Coming soon

FRAME

Year 2009
Builder. . . . . FNA Custom Cycles
Type . . . . Gooseneck drop seat
Welding . . . . Nate Rayburn
Rake. . . . . 38 degrees
Shocks. . . . . Ride Rigid
Modifications . . . . Yup!

This is the only chain-driven R75 custom the author came across.

WHEELS

Front

Size	23in
Wheel	1979 XR 500 32 spoke
Tire.	Bridgestone
Brake.	Drum

Rear

Size	18in
Wheel	Custom Chrome
Tire.	Pirelli
Brake.	Brembo on diff

ACCESSORIES

Bars.	FNA SS Boardtrackers
Handlebar controls	1979 XR 500
Fender	Led Sleds
Headlight	1976 Honda Elsinore 175
Tail-light	1924 Ideal Rode light with FNA mods
Speedo	1966 BMW R60
Dash.	Tank
Front pegs	FNA
Rear pegs.	Fell off
Electrics	FNA
Gas tank.	2000 FXDWG/FNA
Oil tanks.	Internal
Oil system	Sump-fed
Seat	FNA/Farr
Sissybar	FNA
Mirrors	Right, round
Grips.	Oury

Let's tear up the beach!

Carburettors are from a 1982 Yamaha Vision 550.

The steering head was altered significantly to lower the BMW and make room for the long and narrow springer fork, although this narrow fork meant a front brake could not be fitted. The rear shocks got scrapped in order to make the rear of the frame rigid. The bike also has home-made footrests, and the motor is an original 500cc BMW, according to Bogner, the former owner.

An interesting BMW chopper in Texas.

Thorsten Behren's chopper from 1982-1984, Germany (R50/2 from 1969, with R69 engine from 1959) ...

... and this is how the bike looks today. Very versatile hardware indeed!

Another custom paint job by Slavko Sekulic, Serbia, this time on an R75.

A close-up of the gas tank.

The dark color scheme continues onto the rear fender and shock absorber housing.

Fran-6, from Milwaukee Belle in France – the yellow chopper

Fran-6 started this chopper from nothing, using spare parts found or bought here and there. In fact, he kept only two small items of the original BMW frame: the two lower sections with the hardware for the engine and the stand mounts – everything else he fabricated himself. The engine is a 650cc unit. Fran installed bigger intake pipes on the heads because he thought the original carbs were ugly. The rest of the bike specs are in Fran-6's own words:

"Air intake: handmade 60mm diameter with small air filter inside plus water deflector. Exhaust pipes: handmade 60mm diameter with good muffler inside (handmade too). I knew in advance these exhaust pipes would be powder coated, so I built a 'double-pipe' tubing (inside the big one, there's a smaller one) to protect and save

Fran-6's chopper, with its distinctive air intake pipes.

The small jockey shifter you can see on the left of the engine is directly connected to the foot shifter.

the powder coating from burning. Gearbox: five-speed and kick-start. Battery: in the black box under the gearbox. There's another jockey-shifter at the rear left of the frame. Tires: classic 21in and 16in. Lacing: myself. Fork: 160mm extended, believed to be from a police model ... can't remember. The front fender is, in fact, a strong piece, keeping the two arms together. Headlamp: minimalist (I sleep at night). Under the headlamp cover is the horn (from a small scooter). Front brake: master cylinder and Lockheed cup. Ignition: Honda Dax.

"All electrical wires, and clutch cable and throttle cables are in the frame tubings. The tank was started from an old Sportster tank. New and deeper tunnelling and real stretch, and original BMW gas filler. The tank is directly welded onto the frame (tank bolts suck!) – there's a

This chopper is certain to attract attention at the local bistro.

A lovely piece of rolling art.

second one under the seat! Total capacity of both: 7.5 litres (pheewww!) The upper and lower tanks are connected by a hose under the saddle. Frame, handlebars, rear fender, etc: home-made. I have built this bike as smooth as possible, shaving most original cooling fins I found (even on the front hub). All you see black is powder-coated; all you see yellow is paint.

"The biggest problem with this low-low-low-rider was the driving, not the handling! The foot controls and rider's position ... If you take a look at the foot controls, you'll see they all operate with the heel, gearchange and rear braking. For me, the riding position was exactly what I wanted: kind of 'jockey,' sitting with my arms straight forward.

"About the foot controls: once you've entered this new operating mode in your head (it's hard in the beginning), there's absolutely no problem. I made hundred kilometers without any difficulty! The BMW motor was fun to hear, I loved the way it whistled when accelerating (due to the intake pipes). The scoot was glued on the road and it was easy to ride without hands, like on rails! This scoot was happiness ... and happiness ... and happiness again. I'm completely mad about the shape and colors, absolutely NO noise or nervousness, speedy, easy handling, marvellous brakes, always starting at the first kick ... I have had other scoots, even Harleys, but the one I keep on dreaming about today is this one."

A beautifully stretched out hard-tail custom BMW.

Gyuri Petik, Hungary/UK – Silent Scream R65

Gyuri and his dad built this chopper a couple of years ago. They changed a lot of parts on the bike, bar the engine (BMW R65 LS, 1981) and transmission. The frame was home-made, using gas pipes. The fenders and the seat frame are made of fiberglass. The front brake disc is a Jaguar car disc with Brembo callipers. The most difficult task was to incorporate the shaft drive into the design.

All parts were made individuallly; hence this BMW is absolutely unique.

The gas tank is from a Honda Shadow 750.

Bottom left: The wheels came from an old Jaguar E-type.

The front fork is made from Husaberg parts.

Part two: airhead bobbers

Sylvain Valin, France

Sylvain designs virtual motorcycles; he's also a rider and web surfer.

In his blog Sylvain showcases standard bikes and the changes he's made to them in his virtual design: myspace.com/sylvsdesign.

Sylv's design, below, is based on BMW's R51/2 from 1950.

Very nice indeed!

Frank Staegert, Germany

Frank likes to change things regularly. The bike has also had a café racer appearance in the past.

The current features are: Harley Sportster gas tank, forks shortened by 6cm, addition of Tomaselli Cross handlebars, shortened front fender, rims powder-coated in black, Koso digital speedo fitted, shortened rear frame, rear fender from Triumph, Dunlop Trailmax tires, addition of a 2-into-1 exhaust, airbox removed and replaced with two K+N filters, Honda Fireblade ignition coil, and chrome parts blackened.

Frank bought his BMW 18 years ago and is still fine tuning it. He is happy to work for others planning to do the same.

Frank can be contacted at stahlhuette.design@t-online.de.

Bullseye indicators are very much in fashion on German customs.

The matt black paint job is a current trend.

Bike features a shortened rear frame and fender.

Boxer Schmiede, Germany,
www.boxerschmiede.de

This cool R75/5-based turbo boxer comes from a workshop in Berlin. Charlie's bike started out with a rigid frame and was later converted to have rear suspension. The engine is from an R100S, the paintjob in traditional silver smoke.

The Turbo Lo Rider. (Courtesy MO Medien, Germany)

This bike produces 139hp at 7500rpm and weighs 181kg. (Courtesy Stefan H Schneider)

Although not a chopper/bobber, the bike on this page – built and owned by Georg Bayer – is an interesting mix of old and new.

This bike was named an R1100/5.

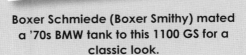

Boxer Schmiede (Boxer Smithy) mated a '70s BMW tank to this 1100 GS for a classic look.

It is a sport/racing boxer with a dry weight of 181kg.

Mark van der Kwaak, Holland

Here is Mark's story:

"Way back when I was 18 years old, the first bike I put together myself was a 1951 BMW. Back then I wanted a Harley but could not afford one, so I put that Beemer together, all black and chrome and pretty, and before I had a chance to ride it, I got an offer to trade it for a 1969 Norton Commando, in boxes. The Norton was a 750 with papers, and the BMW was a 500 without papers ...

"I fixed the Commando, sold it, and bought my first Harley – a 45in flathead WLC. I loved that bike! When I was 21 I bought a Shovelhead, and I rebuilt that bike every winter until pretty much all of it had been modified at least once. I still have that Shovel, by the way, but I kept thinking about that old Beemer, too. A couple of years later I was able to buy a crashed BMW R90/S for about $400. The bike was in terrible shape, as it had hit a piece of concrete curb and landed in a canal. It had been dredged up the next day and dumped in a shed where it sat for six years. When I bought it there was still canal water in the engine and gearbox.

"I bought an old 1951 BMW R51 frame at a swap meet; the neck had been raked to put a 10in overstock Honda fork in it. I took it apart and repaired the engine and gearbox of the crashed R90/S, and put them in the R51 frame, and, using all sorts of parts I had collected over the years, I built myself a BMW ratbike. It had a Benelli front wheel, DKW headlight, Honda fork legs, Harley trees, and so on. I painted the whole thing army green and rode it like that until August of 2005.

"I decided to put a Springer fork in it, so the neck on the frame needed to be de-raked and moved forward a bit. Once we had the frame in a jig we noticed that it was pretty warped, although I never really noticed it while riding. I decided to change the plans and build a hard-tail frame then.

"What I really loved about the old BMW frame was the fact that it had oval tapered tubing in the front downtubes and under the seat, so we kept those pieces and built the rest from scratch. Thanks to my buddy, Ronnie Breuer at Iron Pit, who welded the frame together in his frame jig.

"Somewhere along the road things got a little bit out of hand, as I decided to design my own wheelhubs with long spokes on one side and short spokes on the other. Aad Heemskerk machined them for me, and, of course, the spokes and rims also had to be made. The Springer was shortened about an inch and a half; we made the front brake from scratch using the internal parts from the BMW R90/S wrecked bike. The gas tank is a heavily modified Superglide tank I got for free, the headlight was 10 bucks at a swapmeet, the fender home-made, the seat a modified Crime Scene Choppers Hardass, tail-light from Crime Scene Choppers, too. (I did the CAD work for most of CSC's cast parts.) The mid-controls are home-made in stainless using Mooneyes exhaust caps as footrests. Handlebars and pipes also stainless, thanks to Aad Heemskerk. The bronze risers are parts that I make and sell on my website (www.dbbp.com). Carbs

This bobber was designed using CAD software.

Opposite: A sneak preview of Mark's bobber.

THE BOBBER	
Owner	Mark 'Duckman' van der Kwaak
Bike name	Cadbike 33, the BMW
City/State	Leiden, the Netherlands
Builder	Mark van der Kwaak and Aad Heemskerk
City/state	Leiden/Warmond
Company info	DBBP-Design, web site: www.dbbp.com, email: info@dbbp.com
Fabrication	Aad & Mark
Manufacturing	Aad & Mark
Welding	Aad
Machining	Aad & Mark

are Stromberg 97s with home-made aluminum manifolds. Instead of cables they are operated by little stainless steel pushrods. Paint is Crème White with Reseda Green, Nicoline painted a German eagle with a duck's head on the front of the engine (from a drawing by my friend at venividivince.com). The bike has no chrome, all the shiny bits are either nickel plated or stainless steel. It was fun to build something other than a Harley for a change!"

ENGINE

Year	1976
Make	BMW
Model	R90S
Displacement	900cc
Builder or rebuilder	Mark
Cases	R90S
Case finish	Smoothed, grit blasted, glass beaded and clear coated
Barrels	R90S
Barrel finish	Black powder coating
Head finish	Grit blasted and then glass beaded
Carburation	Stromberg 97s on home-made manifolds
Air cleaner	Stromberg scoops
Exhaust	Stainless steel by Aad
Mufflers	Stainless steel by Aad

TRANSMISSION

Year	1976 (rebuilt by Mark)
Make	BMW (four-speed with kick-start)

FRAME

Year	2008
Make	Used some oval tapered pieces from a 1951 BMW frame, 60 per cent new
Style or model	Design by Mark
Stretch	6in in the rear
Rake	30 degrees
Modifications	Raised engine mounts, hard-tail, welded together by Ronnie Breuer

FRONT END

Make	Harley Davidson
Model	45in Springer
Mods	Shortened 32mm, rocker nuts home-made in brass

Mark and Aad with their showstopper bike.

A lot of detail went into this bike. Unsurprisingly, it's not for sale.

WHEELS
Front
Make. .. .. Hub – one-off by Aad and Mark, 80 stainless spokes and rim by Haan Wheels
Size 16in
Brake callipers .. .. Drum brake – one-off by Aad and Mark
Tire.. .. .. Firestone
Rear
Make. .. .. Hub – one-off by Aad and Mark, 80 stainless spokes and rim by Haan Wheels
Size 16in
Brake callipers .. .. Stock BMW drum brake with shock mounts shaved off
Tire.. .. .. Firestone

CONTROLS
Foot controls .. .. Stainless steel mid-controls by Aad and Mark
Handlebar controls . .. . Reverse grips
Kickstand .. .. Center stand in stainless steel by Aad and Mark
Electrical wiring . .. . Mark
Headlight .. .. 10 dollars at a swap meet
Tail-light .. .. Crime Scene Choppers

WHAT'S LEFT?
Seat .. .. Crime Scene Choppers, re-upholstered by Paul Funk
Gas caps .. .. Crime Scene Choppers
Handlebars .. .. Stainless steel by Aad and Mark on bronze risers by Mark
Grips.. .. .. Indian (from swap meet)
Pegs .. .. Mooneyes exhaust caps used as pegs
Fuel lines . .. . Copper
Special items .. .. Hardass Seat and Rapide tail-light designed by Mark, together with Crime Scene Choppers
Comments .. .. Not for sale
Credits . .. . Aad Heemkerk, Ronnie Breuer, Ben's Metalshaping, Paul Funk, Nicoline Heemskerk, Venividivince

SHEET METAL
Tanks . .. . .Mark and Aad
Fenders . .. . .Ben's Metalshaping and Mark
Panels . .. . .Engine top cover by Ben's Metalshaping, Aad, and Mark

PAINT
Type . .. . .Cream White with Reseda Green
Graphics or art .. .. .Logo on bike designed by Venividivince, painted with brush and oil paint by Nicoline

Rodney Aguiar, United States

Rodney works for Roland Sands, and has built several very nice custom BMWs. Two are presented here.

Pictured here, the yellow bobber's frame and fuel tank are custom-made, the exhaust pipes are ex-FMF RM250, the front end is from a GSX-R750, and the paralever single-sided swing arm is ex-BMW R1100. Paint and striping are by Mike Maldonado and Jimmy C.

Rodney:

"My whole life I've always been fascinated by movement. It doesn't necessarily have to have wheels to create movement, but they sure add the fun and danger to it. Building motorcycles allows me to purge the thoughts in my mind or release the creative movements of my hands. It is hard to say. I just want to move and create, maybe make people think. Motorcycles are only one venue in which I create movement. Make every moment count and your life will become a work of art."

This bobber is based on a 1983 R80 model.

The paint job complements the bike's overall appearance.

This green custom BMW is based on an R80ST model from 1983.

The tank design took inspiration from 1920s BMWs. (Courtesy pnwriders.com)

John van Dalen, Sionbikers, Holland

This model is an early bobber project.

The black and red color combination works quite well.

John has good reason to smile – it's a nice bike.

Side panels blend in nicely with the overall concept.

This later creation has had the rear frame chopped.

The later BMW bob job ready to roll.

German hard-tail BMW bobber

Rolf Reick's hard-tail bobber, Germany. www.krautmotors.de.
(Courtesy Stephan H Schneider)

This bobber is owned by Rainer Kohl, Kfz Werkstatt, Mannheim, and is
similar to the one built by Rolf Reick; engine is R75/6 of 900cc.

The hard-tail frame is from a World War II BMW R75. The front end is also R75/6, and the exhaust from www.louis.de.
(Courtesy Stephan H Schneider)

William's French bobber

William first stripped a standard bike of all the things that were not needed any more, like the panniers, fairing, crash bars, gas tank, original air box, seat, lights, and various brackets. A friend of Williams' reworked the engine for him, before the bike was returned to him to paint the frame and rims. The small indicators are LED. The exhaust has SITO mufflers fitted. William also owns a café racer, based on an old R80 bike.

The front of the bike has a muscular appearance.

The original bike was an ex-French Gendarmerie machine prior to its bob job. It was an R80RT from 1986 with 100,000km (62,000 miles) on the clock.

The bike has a reworked gas tank from a Honda Shadow.

Mexican single seat.

Air filters are from BMC, and a small headlight is fitted.

The single disc brake on the original bike was swapped for the dual discs from a BMW K75.

Wrenchmonkees

Wrenchmonkees is a motorcycle custom shop, based in Copenhagen, Denmark, which rebuilds and customises old and new bikes.

Wrenchmonkees (www.wrenchmonkees.com) supplied the following: handlebars, levers, grips, rear frame, seat, rear fender, front fender, rear light, front light, steel battery box, wiring harness, and custom paint.

A good place for older BMW parts is www.ulismotorradladen.de (no relations to the author), especially for single-cylinder bikes R24-R27, boxer oldies from 1948-1969, and young-timer R models R50/5-R80GS basic, 1969-1996.

BMW R80 engine	Approx 55hp
Front fork.	Standard
Swing-arm	Standard
Rear shocks..	Gazi Gas
Wheels	Standard – 1.85 x 19 front, 2.15 x 18 rear
Tires	Firestone Deluxe Champion – 4.00 x 19 front, 4.50 x 18 rear

Monkee 9.

The bike has WM megatron mufflers, and an exhaust heat wrap.

CHAPTER 3
BMW OILHEADS
(FOUR-VALVE BOXERS)

The 1200C Classic.

The year 1993 heralded the arrival of the new BMW four-valve boxer generation. The R1100 RS model was the trailer for the new range. This bike combined sports touring, tradition and the latest technology, all in one. One of the main features was the innovative front-wheel BMW Telelever suspension.

With the launch of the R1200C in 1997, BMW entered the cruiser segment for the first time. By the '90s this market had grown into the largest worldwide, with a share of more than 30 per cent of sales. It was not only the boxer engine, but also the design of the R1200C that made this a welcome new cruiser with its own distinctive looks. It could also be toured, in the best BMW tradition.

The R1200C cruiser was initially publicised by a clever pre-launch appearance in the James Bond movie *Tomorrow Never Dies*. The cruiser range was expanded in 1999, and an 850 version was added to the lower end of the range. Further additions were the R850 and 1200C Avantgarde. In 2000, the R1200C Independent was introduced. With its aluminum wheels, abundance of chrome, single seat, speedster windscreen, and two-color paintwork, it was designed as an upmarket model for the range. In autumn 2003, the R1200C Montauk entered the market as another unique model. It rounded off the range between the R1200CL luxury cruiser and the 'basic' cruisers.

BMW decided to discontinue its cruiser range after 2004, due to the trend in the cruiser sector pointing to capacities far beyond 1200cc.

Total production from 1997 to 2004 was 40,218 units.

The 1200C Independent.

The 1200C Independent with optional pillion seat.
(Courtesy Craig Taylor, NZ)

Opposite page: The 1200CL.
(Courtesy Swanie, NZ)

The 1200C Montauk.

Specifications for the R1200C Classic:

ENGINE

Type	Air/oil-cooled two-cylinder, four-stroke boxer, one camshaft and four valves per cylinder
Bore x stroke..	101 x 73mm (3.97 x 2.87in)
Displacement	1170cc
Max power	61bhp (45kW) at 5000rpm
Max torque	98Nm 72ft-lb at 3000rpm
Compression ratio	10.0:1
Fueling control/engine management	Electronic intake pipe injection/digital engine management: Bosch Motronic MA 2.4 with overrun fuel cut off
Emission control.	Closed loop three-way catalytic converter

POWER TRANSMISSION

Clutch..	Single disc dry clutch, hydraulically operated
Gearbox.	Constant mesh five-speed
Gearbox ratios	2.050/1.600/1.270/1.040/0.800:1
Final drive ratio	2.54:1
Final drive	Shaft drive

ELECTRICAL SYSTEM

Alternator..	700W three-phase alternator
Battery	12V/19Ah

CHASSIS

Frame	Three-section composite frame consisting of front and rear section, load bearing engine
Front wheel suspension.	BMW Motorrad Telelever, stanchion diameter 35mm, central strut
Rear wheel suspension .	Die-cast aluminium, single-sided swinging arm with BMW Motorrad Monolever; central strut, spring pre-load mechanically adjustable
Travel front/rear.	144/100mm (5.66/3.93in)
Wheels.	Cross spoke wheels
Wheel rims, front	2.50 x 18
Wheel rims, rear.	4.00 x 15
Tires, front	100/90-ZR 18
Tires, rear	170/80-ZR 15
Brakes, front	Dual disc brakes, floating brake discs, diameter 305mm/12in, 4-piston fixed calliper
Brakes, rear	Single disc floating brake 285mm/11.22in diameter, double piston floating calliper
ABS.	BMW Motorrad ABS

DIMENSIONS/WEIGHTS

Length x width x height	2340 x 1050 x 1130mm (92.12 x 41.33 x 44.48in)
Seat height	740mm/29.123in
Wheel base..	1650mm/64.96in
Castor (in normal position).	86mm/3.38in
Steering head angle (in normal position)	60.5 degrees
Fuel tank useable volume..	17.5 litres/3.84 gal/4.62 gal US
Reserve	4.0 litres/0.87 gal/1.05 gal US
Unladen weight with full tank	256kg/563lb
Dry weight.	236kg/519lb
Max permissible weight	450kg/991lb
Payload (with standard equipment)	194kg/427lb
Fuel consumption over 100km at constant 90km/h.	4.8 litres/58mpg/49mpg US
Fuel consumption over 100km at constant 120km/h.. ..	5.9 litres/47mpg/39mpg US
Fuel.	Unleaded premium minimum octane rating 95 (RON)
Top speed	104mph/168kmph

Grueter & Gut Motorradtechnik, Ballwil, Switzerland, www.gg-technik.ch

In 2000, GG released a custom creation of the BMW factory cruiser – the GG Cruso. Its two models, the GG Cruso Classic, and GG Cruso Sport, met with considerable success around Europe.

The company, based in Ballwil, outside Lucerne, has been designing and building its own machines since 1985. The basis for most of its creations are BMW engines.

GG was commissioned by BMW (Switzerland) AG in 2001 to upgrade the Swiss army's entire new motorcycle fleet to meet the army's specific requirements.

The unique GG Quad, as well as the GG Quadster, and Taurus trike (presented in later chapters), are the logical extensions of the various motorcycles and other vehicles that GG Motorradtechnik developed over the course of the last 20 years.

The Cruso Classic.

Tasteful changes have been made.

The instruments are incorporated into the gas tank.

A view of the instrument cluster from the top.

AME-Chopper GmbH, Schauenburg, Germany, www.ame-chopper.de

Walter F Cuntze and his team are pioneers in the German chopper builder scene. Their business started in 1973 when few people were interested in such motorcycles, and the authorities presented considerable hurdles to getting the bikes onto the road legally.

The firm worked closely with the German TüV as it developed its constructions. It was the first company to build bikes in the best American chopper tradition, and to get them approved and registered on the road.

The first frames the company developed in-house used Japanese inline-four cylinder engines. Today, all engine configurations, including all Harleys, are catered for.

The R1200C Cruiser is the result of collaboration between AME and the successful designer T George. The AME modification has EU approval.

AME-BMW R1200C cruiser
Each of the following assembly groups can be mounted individually.

1. Front end nine-degree rake
Complete kit including fork tubes, bearings, spring-adjusting, three steel braided brake hoses, brake diverter and mounting hardware.

2. Handlebars
Complete kit includes AME handlebars and steel braided clutch and brake hose.

3. Headlight
Rectangular H4, 170 x 110mm, show-chromed with support brackets. Double headlight round H4, 90mm, parallel mount with support brackets.

The AME gas tank, seat, and rear-end combination, with its 200/50-17 tire, and the show-chromed 6in spoke wheel, characterises the AME Cruiser's appearance.

AME's redesigned BMW R1200C.

4. Wheels and tires

Front tire – for original rim: Pirelli 120/80 ZR 18 Dragon GTS or Metzeler 110/80 ZR 18 ME Z4.

Rear: AME custom wheel with aluminium hub, show-chromed steel rim 6.00 x 17 and stainless steel spokes. Tire – Pirelli 200/50 ZR 17 Dragon Corsa,* or Metzeler 190/50 ZR 17 ME Z4.

Complete wheel with tire – just bolt on.

* Inclusive swing-arm modification (swing-arm to be provided).

5. Extra gas tank

Invisible under the seat, additional volume of four litres, stainless steel with fuel pump connected to the main gas tank.

6. Exhaust system 'Super Trapp'

Two-in-two AME-Super Trapp exhaust system, stainless steel, 20-degree rake and EU approval.

7. Gas tank/monocoque/seat/front fender

Complete assembly unit including:
- Steel gas tank (in exchange for original gas tank), 13-litre volume with electric fuel pump
- Monocoque with integrated tail-light, ground-coated GFK
- Front fender
- Stainless steel rear signal brackets with show-chromed 'bullet lights'
- Choice of seats with no extra cost – 'Gunfighter' (as shown) or original BMW driver's seat (to be provided), adjusted to the original BMW sissybar-luggage rack-rear seat unit

Original tires may be used, custom painting optional.

AME-Chopper from Germany, based on a BMW R100/7 engine with an AME chassis from the '70s. (Courtesy Stephan H Schneider)

Norbert's C-Drag
A nice conversion of a factory cruiser.

Modifications to this bike:
- Headlamp: Harley V-Rod
- Tires: front 120/70; rear 180/55 ZR 17
- Sebring exhaust with kat
- Front spoiler: Grüter & Gut
- Digital instruments from Tiny
- Lowered fender from BBS
- LED rear lights
- Kellermann indicators
- LSL handlebars
- Custom paint job

Norbert's C-Drag. (Courtesy www.r1200c.de)

The bike runs on BBS wheels, 3.5 x 17, and 6 x 17.

Randy Smith, FRS Engineering, USA,
www.frsengineering.com

Randy's shop in Murphysboro, Illinois, specialises in custom BMW motorcycle restorations. This particular bike was his first attempt at building a full-on custom BMW, and it turned out to be stunning.

Randy tells the story:

"Building this bike took about two years, working in my spare time (I still had to make a living, you know). I had been restoring old BMWs for about ten years, plus any other motorcycle work that showed up at my door. I purchased a wrecked 1996 BMW R1100RS from my local dealer, and saw that the frame was unsalvageable. I decided a special project was in order.

"After locating a new Harley-style soft-tail frame, I started the major surgery. I removed all the frame insides, and started over to fit the BMW motor and swing-arm. After getting the rear wheel and swing-arm in place, I literally hung the motor in the frame with straps, and fabricated the mounts around it. Since I decided to install carburettors (40mm Bings), I also had to find a suitable ignition system. I was able

Randy's stunning BMW four-valve boxer chopper.

Engine and frame modifications up-close.

to use a Dyna 2000 ignition system made for a GSX-R750. I installed a pick-up magnet into the end of the crankshaft, and mounted a pickup sensor plate under the alternator pulley. I had a machinist build an adapter for my rear wheel, and I used the old BMW antilock brake sensor ring for my speedometer input for the Dakota Digital Instruments. The engine block was re-tapped for all the new oil and breather lines, while I installed all new engine insides (crank, bearings, and oil pump and cam chains). The rear end of the transmission was cut off, and the swing-arm was mounted to the frame. Chris Hodgson from San Jose BMW modified some new 1150 cylinders and pistons so I could install them in the 1100 case.

"With a new clutch and valves, I was ready to put the new motor together, after it had a new metallic silver paint-job. I also added carbon fibre-encased oil pressure and temp gauges on the battery box sides.

"The front wheel is a 21in Avon Venom on a billet aluminum wheel with a six-piston front disc brake calliper. The rear wheel is an Avon Venom 180/18/55 on an 18 x 5 aluminum billet wheel with the original Brembo brake. The brake and turn signal lights are LED controlled by a Thunder Heart solid state wiring harness. I installed an oil cooler under the transmission with 12V cooling fans. I fabricated the lower controls, stainless pipes and baffles. All the welding, polishing and painting was

An aftermarket Harley Davidson soft-tail frame (1984-99 style) was completely gutted and welded back together to mate with the BMW rear swing-arm and motor/transmission.

Randy ready for tearing up the beach.

done by me at FRS Engineering. The rear shock is originally from a 2003 Yamaha R1, with a new Hyperpro spring and RaceTech adjuster. The seat was covered in leather, and hand-laced by Roberti Customs of Huston Texas.

"The bike has been a blast to ride. It tracks straight and true at speed, with no shakes or wobbles. The brakes work well, and the engine power and response increases as it breaks in. It attracts attention wherever I take it. People do a double take when they first see it. They say they haven't seen anything like it before. I thought I would alienate the BMW riders, but the response from them has been overwhelmingly positive. Most of the Harley riders that see it also approve. Most just want to stare at it!"

"Hopefully, you will see more FRS Engineering custom BMW-powered bikes in the future."

Original year, make and model: 1996 BMW R1100RS

ENGINE

Head(s)	Original R1100RS with all-new valves and three angle valve grind by Motorcycle Dynamics Racing
Cylinders.	New 1150cc cylinders modified to fit 1100 case with new high compression 1150cc pistons
Cam(s).	Stock BMW R1100RS
Carburation	(Two) 45mm Mikuni HSR
Air box/filters	K&N
Crank	New
Clutch.	New
Gearbox.	Five-speed BMW R1100RS modified to fit frame
Ignition.	Dyna 2000 from a Suzuki 750 modified to work with BMW engine
Exhaust	Stainless steel by FRS Engineering
Oil cooler and lines	12-pass oil cooler from a Honda ATV, with Earl's braided stainless lines and aircraft style fittings; two 12V high output fans for extra cooling
Power output.	The 'Butt' dyno estimates about 100hp+

FRAME

Original year, make and model . .	Aftermarket Harley Davidson soft-tail frame (1984-99 style), stock rake and stretch
Modifications	Frame completely gutted and welded back together to house BMW rear swing-arm and engine/transmission
Footrests and controls.	Foot peg, brake and shifter mounts were fabricated and relocated behind the engine cylinders

FRONT END

Forks	Harley-style wide glide front end with chromed billet triple trees and lowers
Wheel	21in billet Chrome Horse polished aluminum cut-out swept design, with Avon Venom tire
Discs	Polished stainless steel cut-out swept design to match wheel
Callipers.	Six-piston polished billet aluminum brake calliper
Brake lines	Russell stainless steel braided
Handlebars	Drag style Fat Bars drilled for internal wiring
Master cylinders . .	⅝in polished billet front master cylinder and controls
Switchgear	Hurst mini switch housings (old-style Harley type)

REAR END

Swing-arm	2003 BMW R1150R rear swing-arm
Shock	Rear monoshock is from a 2003 Yamaha R1 with an upgraded Hyperpro spring and RaceTech adjuster; shock was modified to handle the extra weight
Wheel	18 x 5in Chrome Horse cut-out, swept design, polished billet aluminum with special steel adapter to bolt to BMW differential; rear hub cover and spinner are from a Chevrolet Corvette wheel
Disc	Stock BMW stainless steel disc
Calliper	Polished stock Brembo calliper
Master cylinder.	Don't know who made it – found it in a motorcycle salvage yard and rebuilt it
Torque arm	Stock BMW torque arm

Front tire is a 21in Avon Venom on a billet aluminum wheel with a six-piston front disc brake calliper.

BODYWORK
Front fender . . . . FatKatz F140 Vegas
Gas tank . . . . 4.2-gallon 2in stretched single piece tank, with custom hidden mounts
Seat . . . . LePera single seat, re-covered with wrinkled finished black leather and hand laced by Roberti Customs
Rear fender . . . . West Coast Choppers Tombstone rear fender, with frenched tail-light and licence plate holder

ELECTRICS
Main loom . . . . Thunder Heart electronic wiring harness
Headlight . . . . Headwinds
Tail-light . . . . Custom clear lens LED
Indicators . . . . Chrome bullet clear lens LED (red back, amber front)
Other . . . . Dakota Digital instrument panel for tach and speedo

PAINT
Color(s) . . . . Frame, swing-arm and differential are flat black PPG DAR acrylic enamel; tank, struts and fenders are black PPG DUC basecoat with PPG 2021 polyurethane clear coat; engine is Silver PPG DCC polyurethane topcoat; all parts were primed and sealed with PPG NCP epoxy primer.
Who did the paint? . . . . Randy Smith and Scott Stites

POWDER COATING
Hi-temp ceramic, exhaust pipes and heat shields by Olympic Coatings, Escondido, California

ENGINEERING
What parts? . . . . Frame and engine/swing-arm mounts; ignition system; carb setup; foot and clutch controls, and rear wheel adapter
Who did them? . . . . . FRS Engineering, and wheel adapter by ProRod

POLISHING/PLATING
All chrome-plated engine parts are stock BMW; all stainless parts were fabricated and polished by Randy

Forks: Harley-style, wide glide front end, with chromed billet triple trees and lowers.

Thanks to:
Larry Phillips from ProRod for the wheel adapter and inspiration; Chris Hodgson from San Jose BMW for the engine upgrade info, and letting me pick his brain on all-round performance issues; Scott Stites for all-round support; the guys at BMW Motorcycles of North County in Escondido, CA, for lots of parts.

Dirty Hands Choppers and Bob's BMW chopper project, USA
www.dirtyhandschoppers.com
www.bobsbmw.com

Bob's BMW is one of the oldest BMW motorcycle dealerships on the East Coast of the United States. Greg, from Dirty Hands Choppers, recalls: "I first met Bob Henig (owner of Bob's BMW and owner of the bike) at the Mid-Atlantic Motorcycle Show in 2007. We had some bikes on display there and I asked if he had any 'shin burners' around that I could cut up. Bob asked if I was serious and we agreed to meet the following week to discuss building a bike. Bob provided me with a 1999 BMW R1200C that was wrecked and had front end damage, but the drive train was intact.

"Much of the bike is handmade and it took almost 11 months to complete the build. Bob's staff were also part of the build.

"On February 6, 2008 we completed the assembly of Bob's BMW. This was good because it was just in time to display her at the Mid-Atlantic International Motorcycle Show on February 8, 2008."

During the building process. (What a fork!)

At the 2008 Mid-Atlantic International Motorcycle Show.

The bike is finished – mission accomplished.

Engine and front end close-up.

65

The Bobschopster ready to pounce.

Engine to rear section close-up.

The concept was to have an ergonomically excellent, highly rideable machine, with as little chrome as possible. This machine will comfortably seat a 5ft 4in rider as well as a 6ft 5in one. It handles exceptionally well, and can be seriously leaned into turns. Even after a few hours, it's still a great saddle to be in!

All images from Bob's BMW and/or Dirty Hands Choppers.

BOBSCHOPSTER

Engine type..	1998 BMW R1200C stock (1198cc) developing 61bhp at 5000rpm; overhead valve, air and oil cooled, fuel-injected with Bosch electronic management
Exhaust	Custom design and construction by DHC
Transmission..	1998 BMW R1200C stock five-speed constant mesh, shaft driven
Forks	Custom design and construction to specs provided by DHC
Chassis.	Custom design and construction by DHC, plus a small section of stock frame
Dimensions	Wheelbase is 10.5 feet or approximately 126in
Suspension	Custom springer front, and stock 1998 BMW R1200C spring and hydraulic rear
Gas tank.	Custom design and construction by DHC
Fenders	Custom design and construction by DHC
Seat	Custom design and construction by John Longo (USA 301-762-4373)
Wheels.	Stock rear from 1998 BMW R1200C (170/80-18in rear) and stock front wheel from a 2008 BMW F650GS Dakar (300-21in)
Electronics.	Minimalised stock electronics, with re-done ignition switch utilising a 1975-94 style three-position switch, Bosch management for engine and fuel injection
Any special features	Plenty! All bodywork and wheels covered in artistically applied black bedliner, back-bone of frame has multiple see-thru tubes, twin PIAA driving lamps, gas cap, and base removed from 1976 BMW

Rear view of the bike.

De Chaves Garage, Spain,
www.dechavesgarage.com

Pablo Gonzalez de Chaves and Carlos Beltran's D1200R is a prototype with a double link front suspension system, and a BMW R1200 boxer engine. The project began with the objective of developing a new suspension system, and finished with the design of the complete bike. The whole process took over a year, aided by 3D computer modelling. The steering is direct (no cardan joints or rods are used), and with a one-to-one turning ratio. Also, the front vertical arm to which the other two horizontal arms reach does not turn; this provides greater rigidity in the complete system, but also makes the complete system more complex and heavier.

The objectives of the build were improved stability and avoiding the uncomfortable front-end dive during braking on bends. For space reasons, a braking system from a Buell XB12 was installed, even though the ABS system of the original BMW was maintained. The oscillating arms of the suspension are mounted on bushings – however, in a revision of the system, they will be mounted on ball joints, which will allow small misalignments in the assembly to be corrected, and the facility for regulation of the rake angle.

The steering is comprised of a telescopic tube that transmits the turning force through torsion scissors. This telescopic tube passes through the front vertical arm to the stub axle, which carries the wheel.

The D1200R is a prototype with a double link front suspension system.

Track testing.

The D1200R chassis is aluminium 7075. Due to the new suspension system, a new cupped front wheel had to be designed.

Stellan Egeland, Sweden. www.seservice.se

Stellan's creation, named Harrier, took third place in the metric class, and fourth place in the freestyle class in the 2009 World Championship of Bike Building. The bike was created from a BMW R1200S.

Stellan: "The Harrier is the first bike in SE Service's new line of modern customs. As with all of our ground-up customs, we have put the focus on visual technique and an exciting riding experience. The purpose of the air scoops on the fuel tank is to supply the space between the muffler and the seat with cooling air, and to give support to the legs while attacking corners."

This is not a show bike, a street fighter or a sports bike. It's the Harrier!
(Courtesy Horst Roesler: www.motographer.de, Frank Sander: www.thunder-media-service.de and www.amdchampionship.com)

View from the top.

The under-seat exhaust setup.

The bike is equipped with ISR's radial brake callipers at the rear wheel, and dual radially mounted, six-piston monoblock callipers in front.

The ISR steering hub is controlled with push-pull cables from the steering head.

Close-up of the steering head and steering cables.

IMME 1200

The IMME 1200 concept bike, based on the BMW 1200 boxer engine, was the creation of Nicolas Dubar and Yves Dufeutrelle, two French design students of the International School of Design.

Although a sports bike in nature, it is fitting that it be shown after Stellan's Harrier concept. The name IMME comes from a now-extinct German motorcycle manufacturer, which built the Imme R100 in 1948. Back then, it was an unconventional design in every respect. The new IMME 1200 is no exception. The concept bike can have all its road legal parts, like licence plates, lights, and mirrors, removed with the ignition key, making the bike's 150hp ready for the track.

BMW helped in the creation of a prototype for the 2006 Intermot Motorcycle Show in Cologne.

The bike was awarded the design contest's Special Prize by the jury.

Snake BMW

These pictures, courtesy of Parolin Denis, show the so-called Snake BMW from Cas Racing, Spain. It was on display at the Padova Bike Show, Italy in 2006, where it won an award, and it is based on a BMW R1150 RS.

The bike has a new chassis and alternative front suspension, while retaining the Paralever rear.

Tires are Avon on braided rims, the rear on 330/30-17.

Lo Rider

BMW unveiled its factory custom concept in November 2008, at the EICMA motorcycle expo in Milan, Italy.

The bike, as presented in Milan, has a post-modern bobber look about it. The concept is such that this is just one of many possible looks. The idea is that the customer designs his own bike at the point of purchase, choosing anything from a bobber to a retro racer to a naked muscle bike, based on a modular platform. BMW would enable a prospective buyer to pick from various options, such as low- or high-mounted exhausts, solo or dual seats, and multiple headlamp options and paint schemes.

Hendrik von Kuenheim, BMW Motorrad's president, said that there are no immediate plans to build this machine, but if response is exceedingly positive, production is very much a possibility. So far, applause and anticipation has come from a diverse range of BMW enthusiasts, as well as from other camps in the motorcycling fraternity in Europe. BMW now wants to test public reaction in the United States before giving the project the green light for production.

Which one takes your fancy?

The Lo Rider is an exciting new concept bike from BMW.

Exhaust options would allow high- or low-mounted versions.

Different paint and seat options would also be available.

Can't wait to see it on the road!

The modular platform would allow customers to design their own bike.

Reaction to the concept bike has been very favorable in Europe.

Panda Moto, France, www.pandamoto.fr

Jean Luc Dupont from Panda Moto, not content with waiting for the BMW factory to decide if the Lo Rider should be produced, swiftly developed his own version of the theme, naming it 'Le Rider.'

The bike is based on the R1200R, with extensive modifications to the suspension, brakes, exhaust system, seat unit, and bodywork.

The wheelbase is adjustable and the wheels are from an R1200GS, with upgrade options to Oehlins suspension and Behringer brakes.

CHAPTER 4
BMW DERIVATIVES

This chapter showcases Russian engines in choppers/bobbers, and Chinese-built Chang Jiang customizations.

Ural motorcycles, Russia

In 1939, during the USSR's prewar preparations, a meeting was held at the defense ministry to determine which motorcycle model was most suitable for the Red Army. It was decided that BMW's R71 most closely matched the army's requirements. Five R71 motorcycles were smuggled to Russia and copied. The Russian version was coded as an M72.

In 1941, a factory was set up in Moscow to produce M72 sidecar motorcycles. It was soon relocated to Irbit in the Ural Mountain region, far away from any possible German bombing raids. The name IMZ stands for Irbit Motorcycle Works. The main bike models built today are the heavy-duty Ural sidecar motorcycles, some export solo bikes, and the custom Ural Wolf.

Dnepr motorcycles, Russia

The Dnepr was known in the Ukraine as KMZ, which stands for Kiev Motor Works. KMZ started its operation in 1950, and changed its name to Dnepr after the river that runs near Kiev. The Dnepr bikes were designed by Ural engineers and used for military production. At first, M72H models were produced, and, later on, the K750 model. The Dnepr factory closed its doors in the 1990s.

Chang Jiang motorcycles, China

This factory is owned by, and is part of, the Hongdu Group. Its CJ750M1 is essentially a copy of the Russian military M72M. Production of its sidecar motorcycles commenced in the late 1950s in Nanchang, with technical support from the USSR.

The BMW R71 is the spiritual ancestor of all Russian and Chinese derivatives. (Courtesy Menoshire)

Russian-built motorcycles

The Ural Wolf factory custom, www.ural.com

The Wolf factory custom.

Model designation..	IMZ-8.1237
Dimensions (LxWxH)	2530 x 850 x 1300mm/
	99.6 x 33.5 x 51.2in
Seat height	670mm/26.38in
Road clearance	150mm/5.9in
Dry weight..	250kg/551lb
Recommended max speed ..	130kmph/81mph
Engine type..	OHV air-cooled, four-stroke,
	flat twin cylinder
Bore and stroke	78mm and 78mm
Compression ratio	8.6:1
Displacement	749cc
Rated HP at 5600rpm..	40
Carburation	Twin KEIHIN L 22 AA
Clutch..	Dry double disc
Rated torque at 4000rpm	52Nm/38ft-lb
Alternator (14-volt)..	55 amps/770 watts
Starting	Electric and kick-start
Gearbox..	Four forward speeds, shaft drive
Fuel..	91 Octane, unleaded
Tank capacity..	21 litres/5.5 US gallons
Front brakes	Brembo disc brake

Rear brakes..	Brembo disc brake
Ignition.	Electronic
Front suspension	PAIOLI telescopic forks
Rear suspension.	Hydraulic spring shock absorbers
Wheels	Chrome steel spokes and cast
	aluminum hubs, front 18in, rear 16in
Color.	Black

The Wolf features Keihin carburettors, Brembo brakes, and Paioli forks. (Courtesy Paul Nitzke)

The Wolf stems from an unconventional union between the Ural factory and the Russian Night Wolves biker club. (Courtesy Paul Nitzke)

HydroKustom, Moscow, Russia, hydrokustom.ru

HydroKustom is a young workshop that emerged with the building of the Woody bike in November 2007. The staff consists of Professor, Axel and Koshey. Axel and Professor started building bikes in the mid '90s, and Koshey built his first bike in 2004.

The Thumb bike took the Russian Custom prize at the Custom and Tuning Show 2009.

The modified gas tank stems from a Harley Sportster.

Thumb bike. (Courtesy Vlad Lifanovsky/Dmitriy Khitrov)

THE THUMB

Engine type..	KMZ M-72N, cylinder head covers modified by HydroKustom
Exhaust	Loud pipes, HydroKustom
Transmission..	KMZ Dnepr MT-10-36, final drive from Ural M-62, cases modified by HydroKustom
Forks	KMZ M-72N
Chassis..	Hard-tail frame
Dimensions	Length – 2200mm; wheel base – 1570mm; seat height – 670mm; clearance – 120mm
Suspension	Hard-tail
Gas tank..	Sportster 2.4 gallons, modified by HydroKustom
Fender	HydroKustom
Seat	Lepera Solo Seat 100, modified by SpeadFreaks (http//speedfreaks.ru), seat suspension from M-72N, modified by HydroKustom
Wheels..	Two rear Ural Wolf wheels, modified by HydroKustom

SPECIAL FEATURES

Carburation	Amal 930, 32mm
Kick-start pedal	HydroKustom, copper plated
Footpegs	HydroKustom, brass
Foot controls	HydroKustom
Handlebars	HydroKustom
Risers	HydroKustom, brass
Handgrips..	Throttle twist grip, Triumph
Pseudo oil tank (contains electrical stuff) ..	Land Rover air filter plus two tractor headlamps, combined by Hydrokustom
Sidestand	Yamaha XV1100 Virago, modified by HydroKustom
Rear brakes..	Brembo from Ural Wolf

Koshey and the Thumb bike.

Modified wheels are from a Ural Wolf.

The Woody took a prize in the Russian Custom nomination at the Custom and Tuning Show 2008, and also went to the Dutch Big Twin bike show in the same year.

Hydrokustom works on any kind of bike (the GSX-R Street Fighter for example), but prefers old-school models.

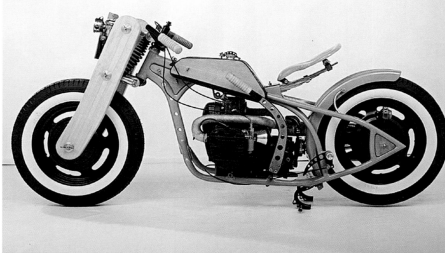

The Woody bike. (Courtesy Vlad Lifanovsky/Dmitriy Khitrov)

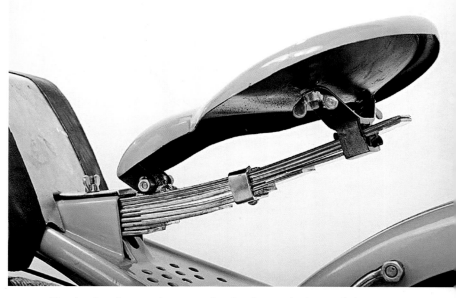

The leaf spring seat suspension is also an in-house job.

Woody's hand-operated gearshift.

Brass inserts on the tank.

The hard-tail frame is the work of Hydrokustom.

THE WOODY	
Engine type..	Ural M-72, front cover, camshaft and magneto ignition from cross Ural, case modified by HydroKustom
Exhaust	Two-into-one loud pipe, HydroKustom
Transmission..	Ural M-72, final drive from Ural M-62, cases modified by HydroKustom
Forks	HydroKustom/DKW NZ-350
Chassis.	Hard-tail frame, HydroKustom
Dimensions	Never measured!
Suspension	Hard-tail
Gas tank.	HydroKustom
Fender	HydroKustom
Seat	HydroKustom
Wheels.	HydroKustom
Any special features	Carbide front and rear lights

Demons of Tranquility, Chaikovsky, Russia, www.dc1859.ru

Three bikes were selected from this outfit's range of Ural bikes. The idea to build the Shark bike came from Oleg Skvortzov. He wanted to build a light frame around a big engine, with the rider sitting right on top of it. The motor used is actually a special 1000cc engine Oleg was able to source on one of his many visits to Irbit, the home of the Ural factory. The Ural plant would have had to change all of its equipment to produce this motor, so the bosses said no, and the project was shelved. Only ten engines of this type were ever produced. Naturally, Oleg was very happy about his find. Vladimir created the frame.

The fuel tank holds 1.5 litres, and is in the engine.

The Shark bike. (Courtesy Dmitriy Khitrov, Roman Wong)

THE SHARK	
Year of build	2005
Engine type	M73, 1000cc
Transmission	Five-speed, one reverse
Suspension	IZH 205
Fuel tank	1.5-litre, in the engine
Frame	DoT
Swing-arm	DoT
Exhaust	DoT
Handlebars	DoT
Front wheel	18in disc made from two IZH discs
Rear wheel	9 x 17in, with 245/40 car tire

Ultra-rare 1000cc Ural engine.

Close-up of the handlebar controls.

On the Motorpark expo in Moscow, Shark won the first place in the Best Russian Bike category.

The next bike from the boys from Chaikovsky is called Chuzhoy.

Oleg before a test run.

Custom-made handlebars.

CHUZHOY	
Year of build.	2006, took seven months
Engine type.	Ural (IMZ)
Tire, front.	140/90
Brake.	Hydraulics (IZH)
Shock absorber	(IZH)
Rear wheel	Pendulum Console, 9(kh)15in
Tire, rear.	225/60
Exhaust	The Resonator
Color.	Gold of the Incas

Front wheel is 4.8 x 15in.

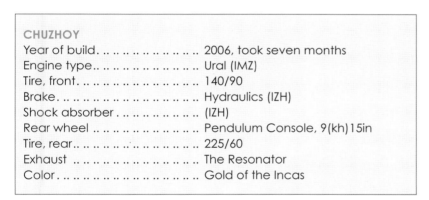

The bike's long and low shape.

THE CALM DEMON

Engine type.. .. ..Ural
Frame .. ..Spinal
Front wheel .. .. ..3.25 x 19in
                    (100 spokes)
Brakes .. ..IZH Orion
Shocks.. .. ..IZH Orion, rear gas
                    oil
Rear wheel 15kh 205
                    (170 spokes)

Front wheel has 100 spokes, and the rear 170.

The Calm Demon.

This classic chopper was completed in 2006 over a period of 18 months.

Dozer Garage, Kiev, Ukraine

Dozer started building bikes as a hobby. He is now 26 years old and wants to build them professionally. He says that not many people in his country know about custom culture, and so the internet is his teacher. Dozer makes many details of the bikes himself, like gas tanks, wheels, frames, handlebars, foot controls, and exhausts.

Readying the engine for the Skull bike.

SKULL

Engine type.. .. ..K750	
Ignition. .. ..12-volt electric	
Carburation . .. .Pacco (mmz)	
Air filter. .. ..Dnepr	
Exhaust system .. .. ..Dozer garage	
Transmission.. .. .. ..Dnepr four-speed	
Kick-starter .. ..Dozer garage	
Frame .. ..Dozer garage, hard-tail	
Gas tank. .. ..Sportster	
Triple tree .. ..Dnepr	
Front ends . .. .Defiant	
Headlight .. ..Custom chrome	
Handlebars .. ..Dozer garage	
Handles .. ..Joker machine	
Sidestand .. ..Dozer garage	
Foot controls .. .. ..Dozer garage	
Seat .. ..Duk Yoly-Paly, NOMAD custom leather parts	
Wing.. .. ..Dozer garage	
Back lantern. .. .. ..Custom chrome	
Brakes .. ..Chinese mopeds and motorcycles	
Wheels. .. ..R21 Dozer garage, R16 Dozer garage	
Spokes . .. .Landmark Twisted	
Tires .. ..Bridgestone	

Skull took Dozer ten months to build.

The Skull bike before the paint job.

The Skull's frame was made by Dozer Garage.

Gas tank is ex-Harley Sportster.

A nicely executed custom.

The Skull all painted up.

COOLDRUG

Engine type..	Ural 650
Ignition. .., ...	Electronic 12V
Carburation	Pacco (mmz)
Air filter	K&N
Exhaust system	Dozer garage
Transmission..	Dnepr four-speed
Kick-starter	Dozer garage
Frame	Dozer garage, softail
Gas tank.	Dozer garage 15-litre
Triple tree	Dozer garage
Front ends	IZ
Headlight	Custom chrome
Handlebars	Dozer garage
Handles	Dozer garage
sidestand	Dozer garage
Foot controls	Dozer garage
Seat	Duk Yoly-Paly NOMAD custom leather parts
Wing..	Dozer garage
Back lamp.	Dozer garage
Brakes	Chinese mopeds and motorcycles
Wheels.	R21 Dozer garage R17 x 7 Dozer garage
Spokes	Landmark
Tires	Metzeler

Cooldrug took 18 months to finish.

The Cooldrug.

Cooldrug with an industrial backdrop.

Dozer and his creation.

Pavel Brayvo, Russian Federation
www.brayvo.ru

Pavel is an industrial designer who has produced several artists' renditions of Russian-engined bikes. Five of his designs are presented here (the bikes were never actually made in metal). These concept bikes date back to 2005.

A close-up of the engine of the Purple Haze concept.

The Purple Haze concept bike, inspired by the Jimi Hendrix song of the same name.

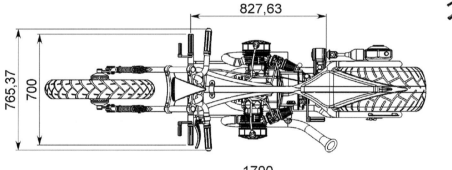

Brayvo Experience

#2 Purple Haze

SIZE	DWG. NO.		REV.
A			
SCALE 1:1	WEIGHT:		SHEET 1 OF 1

Rear wheel 280/R16 and 120-spoke front wheel 130/R19.

The Purple Haze schematics.

Left: The Highway Chile by Pavel Brayvo.
The frame is a BMW suspension-type. Rear wheel 280/R16 Metzeler, and front wheel 130/R17. The rear wheel is belt-driven.

The Selinger. A motorcycle design for my friend Valentina, from Petersburg.

The Blueser. Engine K750, front wheel 80/R19, and rear wheel 170/R16.

Front wheel R21 ...

... and rear wheel R16.

The Remember bike. Both wheels are fitted with 170/R16 Metzelers.

GENERAL
Fabrication .. .. Custom Art
Year/make 2001
Model .. .. Chopper

ENGINE
Year 1998
Model .. .. Ural
Rebuilder .. .. Custom Art
Capacity 650cc
Carburation .. .. 2 x K-68
Air cleaner. .. .. K&N

TRANSMISSION
Modifications .. .. Custom Art

PAINTING
Painter . .. . Custom Art
Color. .. .. Orange-black
Special paint .. .. Gothic

FORKS
Tubes. 36mm
Builder.. .. .. Custom Art

ACCESSORIES
Handlebars .. .. Custom art
Risers . .. . Custom Art
Fender . .. . Custom Art
Headlight .. .. Custom Art
Tail-light .. .. Custom Art
Speedo .. .. None
Electric. .. .. Custom Art
Gas tank. .. .. Custom Art
Seat .. .. Custom Art
Mirrors .. .. None
Engraving.. .. .. Custom Art

Custom Art Orekvovo Moscow

Owned by Sergey Kuzakov and Aleksandr Shiriaev, this highly respected Russian workshop started in 1997. Custom Art has won many prizes for its bikes to date. The workshop builds chopper and bobber bikes, generally American or Russian. The team sees its bikes as being more alive than other brands. Bikes are built to order, and new owners usually become friends. The workshop owners say they love their job, and put their whole souls into it.

The Aivengo ...

... and its gothic paint scheme.

WHEELS
Front
Size . .. . 19 inches
Hub 80-spoke
Tire.. .. .. 90 Dunlop
Brake. .. .. None
Rear
Size 14in
Hub .. .. 80 spoke
Tire.. .. .. 175 Dunlop
Brake. .. .. Disc Orion

FRAME
Builder.. .. .. Custom Art

The Kelt.

The Kelt qualifies for the art gallery.

View from the rear.

GENERAL
Fabrication . . . . Custom Art
Year/make 2003
Model . . . . Chopper

ENGINE
Year 2001
Model . . . . Ural Wolf
Rebuilder . . . . Custom Art
Capacity 750cc
Carburation . . . . 2 x K-68
Air cleaner. . . . . K&N

TRANSMISSION
Modifications . . . . Custom Art

WHEELS
Front
Size 16in
Hub 240-spoke
Tire 130/90
                   Dunlop, H-D
Brake disc . . . . Orion
Rear
Size 15in
Hub 160-spoke
Tire 205/70
                   Goodyear
Brake disc . . . . Orion

PAINTING
Painter . . . . Custom Art
Color . . . . Blue-silver
Special paint . . . . Celtic

FORKS
Tube 38mm
Builder . . . . Custom Art

FRAME
Builder . . . . Custom Art

ACCESSORIES
Handlebars K750
Risers . . . . Custom Art
Fenders . . . . Custom Art
Headlight . . . . Custom Art
Tail-light . . . . Custom Chrome
Speedo . . . . None
Electric. . . . . Custom Art
Gas tank. . . . . Custom Art
Seat . . . . Custom Art
Mirrors . . . . Custom Chrome
Engraving . . . . Custom Art

The blue Ural.

The black Ural bobber.

Stripped down to its essentials.

Side view, and ...

... from the top.

BMW CUSTOM MOTORCYCLES

Bastybikes, Brasov, Romania
www.bastybikes.com

Basty: "My passion for custom motorcycles started six years ago, after I visited Peter Penz custom bikes in Austria. I knew then that I had to start building a motorcycle of my own. After a while, I got in touch with old timers and vintage bikes – that started to get my interest going; combining vintage technology and the custom scene. Later on I saw the 'far-east samurai choppers' ... this is how I started to do what I do today."

Engine and seat unit.

The Rising bike in the making.

Front wheel close-up.

THE RISING BIKE	
Frame	Bastybikes hand-crafted
Fork.	Bastybikes hand-crafted
Wheels, front	19in/Victoria 400 ('50s/'60s original type
Wheels, rear.	15/170/Avon Road Runner
Transmission.	Cut cardan drive with rebuilt parts
Engine type.	Dnepr 650cc with black finish, Bastybikes valve covers
Carburation	Amal, with custom air intake
Tank	Modified '60s Zundapp moped
Fender	Hand-crafted, with hand-forged struts

At the Padua bike show, Italy. (Courtesy Carlo Di Raimondo, www.kustomgarage.it)

A well-deserved Expo entry, Rising is a 100 per cent hand-crafted bike, from the frame right down to its finest details: seat, handlebars, kick-starter, battery box, exhaust pipes, stoplight, hand-forged fender struts, and hand-forged sidestand. The suicide shifter was hand-cut out of a skateboard. Pinstriping was done by Zoliart.

This is another of Basty's bikes, called Battle Without Honour.

Husar Cycles, Poland,
www.husar-cycles.pl

Zwierzak: "I bought my first airbrush in 1999, and started painting bikes as a result of my interest in motorbikes and art. The idea of Husar Cycles came to my friend Nuka and me around 2002, and in 2003 we started together with our project – the Junak low rider. It was still just an idea – there was no workshop. Nuka worked in his garage, and I painted bikes and worked on my bike in my garage. After the low rider was finished, Nuka moved to a bigger town. For almost four years I had been painting Husar motorcycles. In 2007 I started this project again with one of my friends, Strychu, an electro-mechanical engineer. Together, we've done a lot of restorations, such as Russian classic bikes, some BMWs like R12, R35, or the M72 with BMW R80 motor, and also some different custom projects, eg 1986 Shadow chopper, AWO Simson chopper, my Ural bobber, and a sidecar for Royal Enfield. Mostly, I do the airbrushing, but also a lot of sheet metal work, stainless accessories, and so on."

The bike in the making.

All painted up and ready to go.

Engine with forward controls.

Hard-tail frame and sprung seat.

Classic ape hanger handlebars.

"I built this bike initially just for myself, because I always wanted a classic hard-tail chopper/bobber. I'd been riding Russian bikes for 15 years and suddenly, one day, I decided to sell it. The new owner, Tymon, became a friend of mine, so I think he's rather satisfied with my production!" – Marcin 'Zwierzak' Mazur

CAUCASIAN BEAVER
Builders/owners
  name and location. .. .. Husar Cycles, Koszalin, Poland
Present owner. .. .. Tymon
Engine type.. .. .. Ural boxer 650cc
Exhaust .. .. Stainless, handmade by Husar Cycles
Transmission.. .. .. Cardan shaft
Forks .. .. Ural, shortened a bit
Chassis. .. .. Hard-tail, made by Husar Cycles
Gas tank. .. .. Iz 49
Fenders .. .. Handmade by Husar Cycles
Seat .. .. Handmade by Husar Cycles
Wheels. .. .. Rear 15in 140/80, front 16in 130/80
Special features .. .. Painting and ape hanger by Husar Cycles

Chinese-built Chang Jiang motorcycles

Thomas Koehle, Beijing, China
www.4444-chang-jiang-design.com

Thomas has the Chang Jiang bug. He owns three of them; two are highly customised solos, and one is a sidecar version.

Thomas: "I have been riding motorbikes since I was 16, but stopped when I got married at 23. I restored two old cars (one sports car and one WW2 Willys Jeep) but always wanted to restore and build up my own motorbikes.

"I have been working in China since 2005, and discovered the Chinese bike scene with the old-style Chang Jiangs. These are manufactured based on old BMW drawings identical to BMW's R71.

"I moved to China in 2007 and bought my first Chang Jiang sidecar. I modified the stock sidecar with special parts, but this wasn't enough. I wanted something different, and started to collect custom parts like the footboards, tail-light (old Ford), etc, from all over the world for the black bobber bike. Meanwhile, I built up a new solo, but in an old-school style, like old Harleys with winged fenders.

"The old-style Beemers of the bike scene here in China are usually driven by expatriates. The locals are not that much into old stuff, instead buying newer and more modern bikes. Due to the poor availability and high prices of custom parts here, customising bikes is not as popular as in the rest of the world.

The Black Widow solo bike has had the following changes:
- Handmade customised fenders, front and rear
- New headlight
- Ford model A tail-light, with relocated licence plate holder
- Handmade seat with seat springs
- Harley footboards with support frame
- Custom instruments
- Custom turn indicators
- Relocated lock
- Relocated battery
- Relocated rear brake pedal
- Frame transformed from sidecar bike to solo bike
- Custom exhausts
- Powder-coated rims
- Engine is standard, with 24hp

"For the last two years, I have organised motorbike trips through the whole of China with these old repro BMWs. There have been no major breakdowns so far.

First up, the standard Chang Jiang, a nice picture taken by Tony Salvatore.

Thomas' black custom and the sidecar bike.

"The Chang Jiangs are available with 32 or 24hp – recognisable by the shape of the valve covers. Performance of the 32hp engine is not remarkably better than the 24hp, but overall the smaller engine is more reliable than the 32hp engine.

"The black bobber is now approximately ten months old, with 4000km on the clock, and no remarkable defects yet. The bobber is approx 150 to 200kg lighter than the full sidecar, so no wonder

engine performance and reliability is quite good. The build-up took roughly three months to complete. I don't like too many chromed and polished parts, and so I decided just to chrome plate and polish a few small bits and pieces, rather than do a full polishing job."

The Black Widow.

The Black Widow in action in the Chinese countryside.

Thomas posing outside the Olympic rowing park.

Customs in China.

CHAPTER 5

BMW FOURS

The BMW K series, affectionately named 'the bricks' by some, was launched late in 1983. Initially, three variants were produced: the K standard, the K RS (or sport touring), and the K RT (touring version), all with the 987cc four-cylinder water-cooled engine, positioned lengthwise in the frame. Later on, the K1100 variants appeared. I've come across few BMW K custom bikes over the years.

Bastiaan Engelberts: "I bought the 1985 BMW K100RS (below) about a year ago, and I use it every day for travelling to and from work. When the speedometer broke (it was full of water) a few months after I bought it, I decided to build my own from a Sigma cycle comp and a few little lamps. That was the beginning of the transformation. I removed the fairing, changed the mirrors, headlight, blinkers, tail-light,

moved the ignition lock to the side, used some tear plates for covers (front, side and back), added blue LED strips along the backside, cut off the end of the subframe, moved the licence plate, and, of course, I painted it matt-black (with a few white tribal skulls on it). In the future, I want to cut off a piece of the front fender to make it smaller, and maybe change the exhaust ..."

The yellow sport K100 below is from Evert Stobbelaar, Netherlands. The tank and seat are home-built from thin-walled steel plate. The screen originates from a Kawasaki, the front fork and wheels originate from a Suzuki GSX1100F. The rear wheel has a new solid fitting to the BMW shaft drive, and gives space for a 180 tire. The suspension is home-made, using the spring of a GSX1100F, and is adjustable through a linking system.

This K100RS rat bike is from Bastiaan Engelberts, Netherlands.

This is a home-built machine based on a K100LT of 1988.

The matt black treatment.

The frame was built from CrMo pipe and sized like the JJ Cobas framework.

Below are some other examples of chopped and changed Ks.

**This K1100 bike has the tank and rear fender from a Harley Davidson.
(Courtesy Visordown)**

The bobber/street fighter category. (A and M Cycle Traders)

Ronny Zachmann, Germany.

The K Café Racer.

Specification – 1100cc, 215kg, 110hp.

The outright custom job – a 1993 K100 custom. (Courtesy Menoshire)

Hans Joachim Maier from Germany received a top grade for his 1987 design student thesis on this BMW K100-engined motorcycle. The bike was tailored around the driver, resulting in advantages in ergonomics and improved aerodynamics. Even though the design is over 20 years old, there is still some freshness about it today.

One might wonder what a BMW K1000/1100 engine would look like in a retro-style package, made to resemble something like a late 1920s Henderson Model KJ four-cylinder motorcycle. Food for thought ... ?

Hans Joachim Maier, Germany – BMW K100 single seater design from 1987. (Courtesy Max Kirchbauer)

CHAPTER 6

BMW TRIKES

BMW CUSTOM MOTORCYCLES

Trikes are becoming increasingly popular in the biking fraternity, especially so in the United Kingdom.

BMW's concept trikes

BMW is toying with the idea of three-wheeled vehicles, and introduced two trike concepts at its Munich museum in 2009. The first concept, called Simple, reminds me somewhat of aircraft design. It is urban dweller transport, geared towards the professional commuter. The second trike is named Clever. Both were specially designed for fuel efficiency. They are light, tilt through corners due to their suspension systems, are protected from the weather, and have room for a passenger to sit behind the rider/driver. The concepts are a long way away from the BMW Isetta of the 1950s.

Powered by a 230cc single-cylinder engine, BMW's Clever concept trike weighs around 400kg. With 17hp and a CVT transmission, it can accelerate from zero to 60kmph in seven seconds.

The Clever has a range of 200km and a top speed of about 100kmph. It is said to be much safer than a motorcycle in the event of a crash. It also comes with seat belts.

The BMW Clever.

The Clever is currently designed to run on natural gas.

The first concept, called Simple.

Humaid's BMW F650 Trike, United Arab Emirates

Right: Humaid's BMW F650 trike – a rare sight. (Courtesy www.bmbikes.co.uk)

Far right: The trike is an ideal desert mount.

Metal Malarkey Engineering, Shropshire, UK, www.malarkeyengineering.co.uk

Metal Malarkey Engineering is a specialist motorcycle design and development company offering a range of motorcycle frames and bespoke component parts.

Close-up view of the frame strenghtening.

SPECIFICATION
- Converted R80 frame, strengthened by stainless brace across cradle
- Ford Escort axle
- Suspended seat, Hagon shock
- Malarkey alloy slab yoke
- Kawasaki forks, twin four-pot callipers
- Stainless braided hoses, fasteners and Keihin silencers

The object was to create a factory-looking, three-wheeled R80. Components were upgraded where necessary.

BMW R80 trike, owned by Alan Robins in the UK.

A Grinnall, UK-built BMW R1200c trike

This trike was designed by Volvo's Chief Designer, Steve Harper. Steve's work complements the styling of the R1200C beautifully. Steve also designed the Scorpion trike, covered next.

(Courtesy Reg McKenna)

Rear view of the Grinnall trike.

John Clarke's Grinnall Scorpion III reverse trike, Australia

John's 1994 Grinnall Scorpion III is one of only two known to be in Australia (the other is/was in Queensland).

The Grinnall reverse trike.

GRINNAL SCORPION 3

Engine type..	.BMW K1100
Transmission..	.BMW five-speed sequential
Front suspension	.Double wishbone
Rear suspension.	.BMW Paralever
Steering	.Centre rack and pinion
Front brakes	.280mm ventilated discs from a Ford Sierra
Back brake	.BMW K series 290mm
Fuel tank..	.25 litres
Chassis.	.Spaceframe, seamless steel tube
Body..	.Fiberglass and Kevlar reinforced polyester
Front wheels..	.Cast aluminium 7in x 16in
Back wheel	.Aluminum three-piece split rim 7in x 16in
Tires	.195/50VR16 Pirelli
Dry weight..	.395kg
Power	.0-110kmph in 5.0 seconds
Top speed	.200kmph+

The donor bike was an R1200C from 1998, to which Alex fitted a Ford Sierra rear axle, and fabricated a rear subframe with independent suspension.

Alex Coldron, United Kingdom

Alex inherited a firm interest in motorcycles and engineering from his dad, and grew up playing in a garage of modern and classic bikes. At the age of 17 he took the opportunity to improve his welding and lathe skills by building a trike alongside his father.

Alex completed this trike in November 2008.

Further fitments were 19in alloy wheels and long stainless steel exhausts.

South Island Trikers, New Zealand

South Island Trikers told me that this was the only BMW in the club. It is now running a 1600cc Toyota engine, as the BMW engine computer decided to go for a bit of a swim and drowned. The cost of sorting it out wasn't justified, and it ended up cheaper to change the motor and gearbox, and extend the frame slightly. I was told that it ran really well while it was powered by BMW.

The three-seater BMW trike in New Zealand.

Frontal view and ...

... artwork at the rear.

Trike Design, United Kingdom,
www.netupandgo.com/hankschopshop

BMW R1150 RT

Engine type.. .. .. .BMW boxer 1150cc
Exhaust .. ..Custom-made with catalytic
converter
Transmission.. .. ..Standard through elite
via a differential unit
Forks .. ..BMW Cantilever with modified
rake for lighter steering
Chassis. .. ..Trike design bolt on chassis
Dimensions .. ..Approximately 5ft wide;
four inches longer than the
standard bike
Suspension .. ..Adjustable preload and
damping on lateral shock
absorbers
Gas tank. .. ..Standard bike
Fenders .. ..Trike design glass fibre
Wheels. .. ..Aftermarket alloy wheels
Any special features.. .ABS

A nice touring trike from the United Kingdom.

Ed Fletcher,
United Kingdom

Ed's 750cc UK-built trike is based on the Ural Wolf. Following on from a motorcycle accident and resulting spinal injury he made the decision to dedicate his working life to fighting solely for the spinally injured. Ed, a director and head of the Spinal Law team of Fletchers Solicitors in the UK, also runs a blog, www.paraplegicliving.com.

Ed riding his trike.

Keith from Custom Bike Designer, UK, www.custom-bike-designer.com

The aim of the Custom Bike Designer Company is to provide a bespoke 3D design service for anyone wishing to view their custom motorcycle ideas before embarking on the actual build. Different versions can be designed – for example, you can see how the bike would look with different gas tanks, handlebars, colors, etc.

Being a biker himself, Keith would like to think he's much more in touch with his customer's demands and needs, and he takes a totally flexible approach to every project. At the time of writing, the company is developing an 'off the peg' method of custom bike design. This will allow customers to select parts from a list; these will then be digitally assembled for the customer, creating a final rendered image of their design. This will significantly reduce the cost to customers.

The trike strikes quite a pose.

View from the top of this ...

... Ural-powered trike design.

Grueter & Gut, Switzerland, www.gg-technik.ch

The Taurus was launched at Moto Life, Milan, Italy, in November 2009.

GG TAURUS

Engine type..	Four-cylinder, liquid-cooled inline
Valves	Four per cylinder
Capacity	1293cc
Power	129kW (175bhp at 9250rpm)
Torque..	140Nm at 8250rpm
Catalytic converter.	Three-way
Gearbox.	Six gears plus reverse
Fuel capacity..	34 litres
Empty weight..	397kg
Overall length.	2190mm
Overall width	1410mm
Top speed	220kmph

Frame	GG in-house construction
Suspension	Front: single-wheel suspension with trapezoid crossmembers in aluminum; rear: GG Swing arm in aluminum
Shock absorbers	Hydraulic with infinitely variable adjustment
Spring travel.	Front 100mm, rear 130mm
Final drive	Cardan with reverse gear
Brakes	Hydraulic, front 270mm diameter, rear 284mm, front floating, rear rigid brake discs
Wheels	Forged aluminum; front 8 x 17in, rear 10 x 19in
Tires	Front 205/40-17, rear 75/30-19
Homologation	Europe/Switzerland: EC homologation for full power
Driving licence	Car or motorbike driving licence

The trike is powered by a 1293cc, four-cylinder, liquid-cooled, inline BMW engine – and it sure looks the business.

The Taurus is the latest masterpiece from G&G in Switzerland, launched at the EICMA Expo in November 2009 in Italy.

CHAPTER 7

BMW QUADS

The quads in this chapter are miles apart from the beginning of quads in their ATV guise. These creations are about high-performance on the road.

Grueter & Gut, Switzerland, www.gg-technik.ch

GG Quad

G&G was founded in 1983, and has many years of experience in the development and manufacturing of its products. In 2004, Walter Grüter built the first street quad with a BMW boxer engine. Casually characterised by Grüter as a 'toy for boys,' the GG Quad is a four-wheeled motorcycle. The emotional driving experience of the GG Quad is unique in every way.

This quad is a green mean machine.

This version provides some luggage storage capacity.

GG QUAD

Engine type .. .. Two-cylinder flat-four
Valves .. .. Four per cylinder
Capacity 1130cc
Power .. .. 70kW (95bhp at 7250 rpm) EU and CH 15kW
Torque .. .. 98Nm at 5500rpm
Catalytic converter. .. .. Three-way
Gearbox. .. .. Six gears, reverse gear
Tank capacity .. .. 18 litres
Empty weight 375kg
Overall length 2220mm
Overall width 1400mm
Top speed .. .. 170km/h EU and CH 100 km/h
Frame .. .. GG in-house construction

Suspension .. .. Single-wheel suspension with aluminum trapezoid crossmembers
Shock absorbers .. .. .. Hydraulic shock absorbers with infinitely variable adjustment
Spring travel. .. .. 100mm front and rear
Final drive .. .. Via a differential unit
Brakes .. .. Hydraulic brakes, 270mm diameter, floating brake discs
Wheel .. .. Cast aluminum wheels
Tires .. .. Front 195/40-16, rear 225/35-17
Authorized use .. .. Germany: unlimited TÜV authorization; Europe: EC homologation (15kW, 100kmph)

Top left: A close-up of the brake and suspension setup.

Top right: Another view of the suspension.

Four-valve boxer engine and oil cooler.

Quads for people with physical handicaps

Following numerous enquiries, the company decided to build the GG Quad for people with a physical handicap. The GG Quad can be customised to individual needs, for example: electric gear change, thumb brake, special running board (in addition to the carrying frame left and right), driver's foldaway backrest, and modification of footbrake (integral left side, with or without electrical operation).

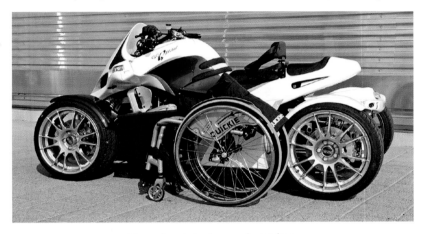

The wheelchair quad version.

GG Quadster

2006 saw the development of the GG Quadster with a BMW K1200S engine, giving more power with the four-cylinder motor. With the homologation in Germany and Europe complete, the first GG Quadsters were delivered in September 2007.

Engine type..	Four-cylinder, liquid-cooled inline
Valves	Four per cylinder
Capacity	1157cc
Power	123kW (167bhp at 10,250rpm)
Torque..	130Nm at 8250rpm
Catalytic converter.	Three-way
Gearbox.	Six gears, reverse gear
Fuel capacity..	26 litres
Empty weight..	390kg
Overall length.	2330mm
Overall width	1430mm
Top speed	210kmph
Frame	GG in-house construction
Suspension	Single-wheel suspension with aluminum trapezoid crossmembers

Precision and speed unite with the GG Quadster.

Shock absorbers	Hydraulic shock absorbers with infinitely variable adjustment
Spring travel.	100mm front and rear
Final drive	Via a differential unit
Brakes	Hydraulic, 270mm diameter floating brake discs
Wheels.	Cast aluminum
Tires	Front 205/40-17, Rear 245/35-18
Authorized use	Germany: TüV approved as a 4-wheel motorbike; EU: EC homologation 15kW

The Quadster has a potent presence.

Martyn from www.autofocusstore.com.au, the distributor of GG trikes and quads in Australia, enjoying the ride.

Pembleton Brooklands

Lastly, this Pembleton Brooklands is powered by a 1000cc, BMW two-valve boxer engine. Although not a quad, this custom car's looks (and performance) are a nice way to bring the book to a close.

John Ward from the United Kingdom built this one, and gives some background information about the car:

"The Pembleton Brooklands comes from designs provided by the Pembleton Motor Company. All that is provided is a chassis and a 15-page manual, and so they are all different. The engine was rebuilt by MotoBins in Spalding, England. The donor vehicle strip started in May 2002, and it took until October to clean and refurbish all of the required parts. The build started in November 2002, and it passed the UK SVA test in March 2004. Under the panel on the rear bodywork are seats and seatbelts suitable for small children, which required some changes to the chassis and panelling when they were made."

The engine comes from a BMW100RT; the rest of the running gear is 2CV.

This is the only four-seater Pembleton Brooklands.

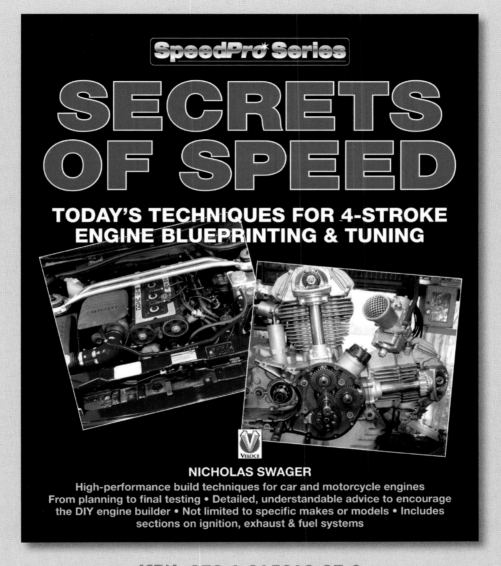

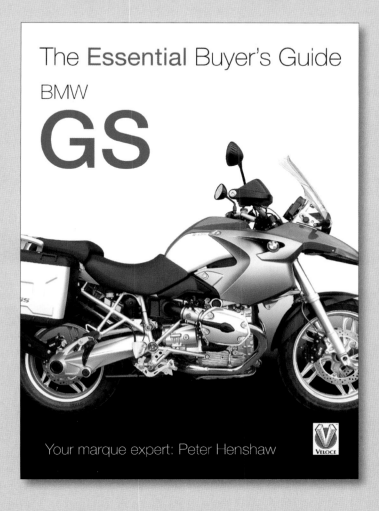

The Essential Buyer's Guide

BMW

GS

Your marque expert: Peter Henshaw

ISBN: 978-1-84584-135-5

Paperback • 19.5x13.9cm • £9.99* UK/$19.95* USA • 64 pages • 100 color pictures

Having this book in your pocket is just like having a real marque expert by your side. Benefit from the author's years of experience, learn how to spot a bad BMW GS quickly and how to assess a promising one like a true professional. Get the right bike at the right price!

For more info on Veloce titles, visit our website at www.veloce.co.uk • email: info@veloce.co.uk • Tel: +44(0)1305 260068
* prices subject to change, p&p extra

Index

—

This index is organized from A to Z in order of countries of contributors: